MUTUAL AID IN THE VICTORIAN COUNTRYSIDE:

Friendly Societies in the Rural East Riding 1830-1914

Hull University Press

Monograph in Economic and Social History

MUTUAL AID IN THE VICTORIAN COUNTRYSIDE:

Friendly Societies in the Rural East Riding 1830-1914

DAVID NEAVE

Lecturer in Regional and Local History
Department of History, University of Hull

HULL UNIVERSITY PRESS
1991

British Library Cataloguing in Publication Data

Neave, David

Mutual aid in the Victorian countryside: friendly societies in the rural East Riding, 1830-1912
1. Yorkshire. East Riding. Friendly societies, history
I. Title
333.7094283

ISBN 0-85958-488-7
ISSN 00783013

Phototypeset in 11 on 12 pt Times and printed by the Central Print Unit, Hull University.

Front cover: Wetherbee, George Faulkner
1851-1920
Haymakers
Designed by John Harmer

Contents

List of Tables and Figures

Tables

Figures

Abbreviations

Abbreviations used for affiliated order names in text

AOF	Ancient Order of Foresters
GUOOF	Grand United Order of Oddfellows
IOOF	Independent Order of Oddfellows
IOOF KU	Independent Order of Oddfellows, Kingston Unity
IOOF MU	Independent Order of Oddfellows, Manchester Unity
IOR	Independent Order of Rechabites, Salford Unity
LOAS	Loyal Order of Ancient Shepherds, Ashton Unity
NIOOF	National Independent Order of Oddfellows
NUOFG	National United Order of Free Gardeners
OST	Order of the Sons of Temperance
UAOD	United Ancient Order of Druids
UOFR	United Order of Female Rechabites

Other Abbreviations

BG	*Beverley Guardian*
BIHR	Borthwick Institute of Historical Research, York
DT	*Driffield Times*
ECH	*Eastern Counties Herald*
HA	*Hull Advertiser*
HN	*Hull News*
HCRO	Humberside County Record Office
HUL	Hull University Library
JRSS	*Journal of the Royal Statistical Society*
PRO	Public Record Office
VCH ER	*Victoria County History East Riding*
YG	*Yorkshire Gazette*

The term East Riding is used throughout the text to refer to the area of the former administrative county and does not include the city of Kingston upon Hull.

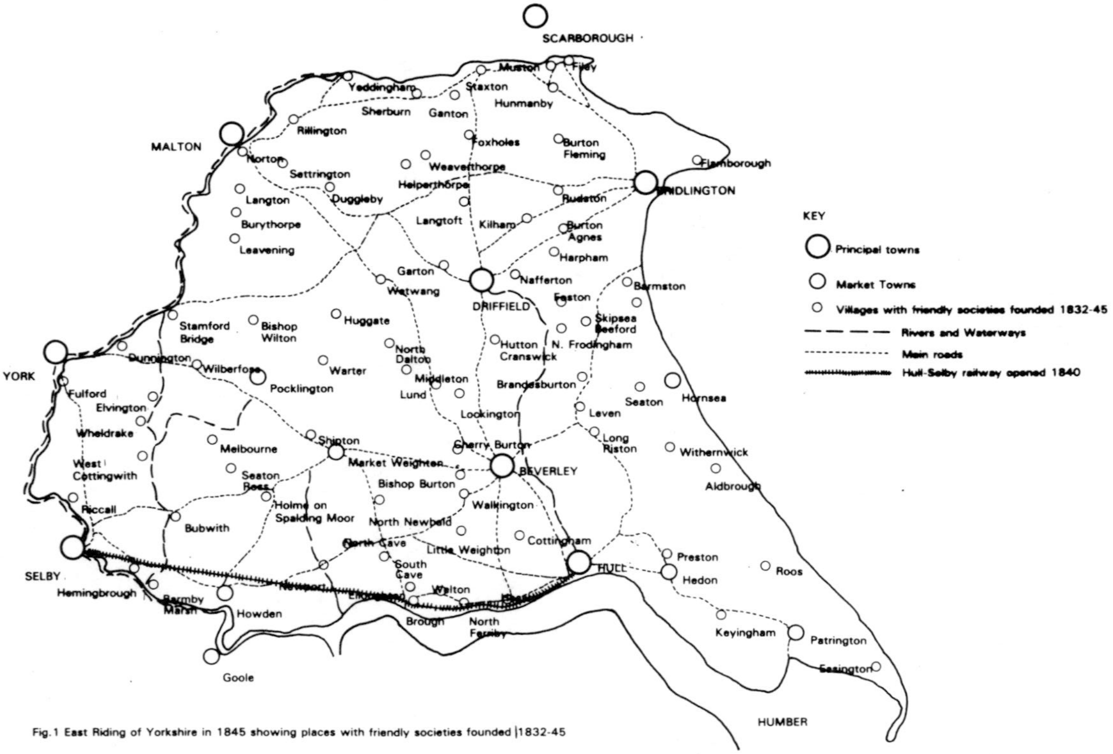

Fig. 1 East Riding of Yorkshire in 1845 showing places with friendly societies founded 1832-45

Introduction

In the late 1830s affiliated order friendly societies with their origins in industrial Lancashire and the West Riding exploded into the rural East Riding. During the years 1838-43 over 100 branches were opened in seventy-five villages providing substantial sickness and funeral benefits for a largely agricultural labourer membership. Further branches were opened up until the eve of the First World War by which time over 250 clubs had been founded in a total of 110 small towns and villages, though not all had flourished. These clubs provided much more than financial relief; for the members there was also the conviviality and fellowship of the monthly meetings and the experience and status of office holding while for the community at large there were the annual feasts which soon became red letter days in the rural calendar.[1]

The experience of the East Riding was by no means peculiar and it has been calculated that in 1891 at least four million male adults in mainland Britain were members of self-managing town and village friendly societies. This figure, which accounts for just under half the male population over the age of nineteen, is particularly impressive when compared with the recorded total membership, in 1891, of trade unions (1,501,083), co-operative societies (1,153,916) and the various Methodist denominations (727,112).[2] Recent writers on aspects of nineteenth century Britain, well aware of the numerical superiority of friendly societies, have variously described them as: 'the major form of mutual organisation among labourers'; 'the one social institution that touched the adult lives of a near majority of the working population'; 'the largest of all the working-class organisations that developed during the period'; and 'the most representative' and 'most widespread of working-class institutions' yet few historians have accorded them more than a paragraph or two.[3] In 1957, in a pioneering article calling for regional research on friendly societies, Eric Hobsbawm commented on how they had been 'surprisingly, and quite unnecessarily neglected by professional historians'.[4]

Thirty years later this neglect is still evident although there are signs of a growing interest in these institutions. In a period which has seen a great increase in the study of labour history and a multiplication of the already numerous works on trade unions, co-operative societies, and Methodism, only two books and a handful of articles devoted solely to friendly societies have been published, the most important and influential of which being P.H.J.H. Gosden's *The Friendly Societies in England 1815-1875* (1961). In this study and in his later wider ranging book *Self-help: voluntary associations in nineteenth-century Britain* (1973) Gosden provides invaluable coverage on the development, organisation, finance, legislation and geographical distribution of local and affiliated societies.[5] He touches on membership and leadership, relationship with the poor law and unemployment and the medical and educational role of the societies but because of his reliance on a limited range of printed and official sources he fails to convey the vitality of individual societies and their importance to the life of the working-man and his community. The existence of Gosden's initial study has meant that since 1961 no-one concerned with nineteenth-century labour or social history has any excuse to ignore what is obviously an institution of far greater significance to the working-class than was considered by the pioneer labour historians of the inter-war years with their concentration on political movements, trade unions and co-operatives.

The writings of E.P. Thompson and Eric Hobsbawm, although rarely dealing directly with friendly societies, have been influential in altering social and economic historians' attitudes and approaches to them. Thompson in *The Making of the English Working Class* (1963) convincingly portrays friendly societies as having a significant role in the formation of working-class culture. He stresses that 'The working-class community of the early nineteenth century was the product, neither of paternalism nor of Methodism, but in a high degree of conscious working-class endeavour' and that it is in the early nineteenth century local friendly societies of northern England that the working man attained the self-discipline and experience in self-government that was vital for the growth of independent working-class culture and institutions.[6] The members of Thompson's early friendly societies were largely 'self-respecting artisans', the very men who were to become Hobsbawm's 'labour aristocracy' in the mid-nineteenth century and it is historians studying this latter group and their role in 'the changes and continuities in the direction and structure of the labour movement, workers' consciousness and social relations between the second and third quarters of the nineteenth century' who have paid particular attention to friendly societies since the early 1970s.[7]

Geoffrey Crossick's *An Artisan Élite in Victorian Society: Kentish London 1840-80* (1978) includes the most detailed regional examination of friendly societies so far published.[8] Crossick rightly points out the neglect in Gosden's study and elsewhere of any full discussion of the membership patterns of friendly societies, their role in working-class life, and their ideological functions and he goes some way to providing important insights into these questions within an urban area. He reiterates contemporary statements which see the affiliated orders as being 'practically closed against agricultural and other unskilled labourers' and the evidence from his particular urban context suggests that they were increasingly socially exclusive providing for the skilled working man a respectable institution of his own within local society.[9]

The themes of respectability and exclusiveness are also explored in T.R. Tholfsen, *Working-class Radicalism in Mid-Victorian England* (1976), and N. Kirk, *The Growth of Working Class Reformism in Mid-Victorian England* (1985). Tholfsen, using official order journals, general laws, lecture books and histories, presents the best published account of the ideology of the affiliated orders in the mid-nineteenth century. He argues that friendly societies, although totally committed to the mid-Victorian social order and its values, did not surrender their independence.[10] They rejected patronage and the 'degradation of charity' but welcomed the approval of the middle classes. Kirk sees respectability as increasingly pursued within the affiliated orders and co-operative societies, as part of an indigenous working-class culture which nevertheless retained beliefs in collective improvement, independence, class pride and the liberating powers of education.[11]

The works cited above are firmly rooted in urban and industrial society and they provide a great contrast to the treatment accorded to friendly societies by writers on nineteenth century rural society who are largely concerned with popular culture. Studies of rural friendly societies are often characterised by descriptions of once-a-year feasting and processions with bands, banners, sideshows and drunkenness involving the whole community and neighbourhood while the town societies are portrayed as exclusive organisations promoting respectability, mutual-aid, education and self-advancement. Friendly societies in the towns are represented as independent artisan institutions sometimes with party political associations while those in the countryside are seen as instruments of social control managed by the respectable classes for a deferential population. This latter view is given full expression in Alun Howkins' detailed study of village club feasts in *Whitsun in 19th Century Oxfordshire* (1973) in which he describes rural friendly societies founded and in many cases run by gentry and clergy who contrived the replacement of the old disorderly Whitsun celebrations by the more rational recreations of a benefit club anniversary.[12] The feast day also figures prominently in Margaret Fuller's *West Country Friendly Societies* (1964) which is particularly concerned with the societies' regalia.[13]

This concentration on the feast day and a romantic folksy image is unfortunately followed in most recent writings on Victorian rural life. Pamela Horn, the most prolific writer on this subject, rarely devotes much space to friendly societies. In her *Labouring Life in the Victorian Countryside.* (1976) discussion of them is relegated to the chapter on 'Holidays and recreations' where two pages are devoted to a rather sugary description of the feast day - 'the real "fete of the labourer" - a day when, for once, he would have plenty to eat and drink and there would be singing, dancing and much laughter'.[14] In defence it must be stated that it is only Horn who gives more than a passing reference to friendly societies in the two volumes of *The Victorian Countryside* (1981) edited by G. Mingay. Here, in dealing with 'Labour Organizations', she briefly comments on the benefits provided by the societies and suggests the importance to agricultural trade unionism of the experience gained by working men in meeting together and running village clubs.[15] This latter point is surprisingly neglected in Alun Howkin's *Poor Labouring Men: rural radicalism in Norfolk 1870-1923* (1985) a work which looks in detail at agricultural trade unionism and Methodism, two of the organisations of the agricultural labourer, yet does not consider the third and largest - the friendly society, although some of his leading figures were active officers of affiliated branches.[16]

The concentration by labour historians on friendly societies as a social movement, and rural historians on their cultural role, has meant that it has been left to historians of social welfare to explore more fully the all important significance of the economic benefits of friendly society membership to the working-man. The nature and extent of the benefits, the attitude of the affiliated orders to state provision of old age pensions and health insurance, and the societies' financial soundness in the late-nineteenth and early-twentieth century are discussed in a number of books and articles, the most comprehensive coverage being in Bentley Gilbert's *The Evolution of National Insurance in Great Britain* (1966).[17] Three recent works concentrate on particular aspects of welfare and medical provision. David Green's *Working-class Patients and the Medical Establishment* (1985) deals with the successful management and extent of working-class medical provision by the friendly societies before, and their loss of control after, the 1911 National Insurance Act; Paul Johnson in *Saving and Spending: the working-class economy in Britain 1870-1939* (1985) looks at the role of friendly society benefits in the economy of the working-class family and Hilary Marland devotes a significant section of her book *Medicine and Society in Wakefield and Huddersfield 1780-1870* (1987) to discussing friendly society provision of medical relief and sickness benefits in two West Riding towns in the mid-nineteenth century.[18] All three works in attempting to provide information on the extent and occupational structure of friendly society membership, matters crucial to their arguments, point to the paucity of sources. Marland records that the 'Evidence on the occupations and social status of friendly society members is unfortunately extremely rare.'; Johnson comments that 'there seem to be few sources' and for Green the evidence is 'patchy' and 'there are no suitable statistics'.[19]

These authors have been handicapped, as have all other writers on friendly societies in the past thirty years, by too great a dependence on printed sources. The printed reports, journals and directories of the affiliated orders have been frequently used but more reliance has been placed on the annual reports of Chief Registrar of Friendly Societies and other relevant parliamentary papers such as the official reports of the Royal Commissions on Friendly Societies 1871-4, Labour 1893, Aged Poor 1895 and the Poor Law 1909. These sources, although containing a wealth of original material, have to be used with caution. The reports of the Chief Registrar are notorious for their inaccuracy.[20] The evidence given to Royal Commissions, although remarkable for its detail, is often conflicting; the comments are frequently impressionistic rather than factual and if used selectively can give a misleading account.

The use of printed sources rather than primary documentary material severely limits both the range and reliability of the research so far carried out. For Gosden in his study 'useful manuscript material' seemed 'practically non-existent' and Hobsbawm thought it unlikely that the local historian would come across many manuscript collections, and others have remarked on the paucity of sources on membership.[21] These statements, however, are misleading for dissatisfaction with what had already been written on rural friendly societies and a desire to discover answers to the many questions posed by Hobsbawm in 1957, coupled with the chance discovery of a cache of records of one village Foresters' club, led the present author to carry out a highly successful search for further manuscript material in the East Riding.[22] Records relating to some twenty branches were located following a limited survey.[23] Nationally the extent of the documentary material must be immense for, although rapidly decreasing in number, there are still hundreds of branches of the affiliated orders in existence and the majority will have records, often going back to the 1830s.

The minute, membership and contribution books of affiliated order branches provide accurate information on the age and occupation of members on joining, the amounts of subscriptions paid and benefits received by individuals, fluctuations in funds and membership, place of residence of members and their mobility, the management of the branch, its involvement with other sections of the community, and the occupational status of the branch leadership.

This study, the first to make substantial use of the records of both individual affiliated branches and the central organisations of the chief affiliated orders, offers a necessary corrective to much that has so far been written on friendly societies and contributes a considerable amount of new information. From a range of national and local sources it has been possible to compile a fairly comprehensive list of affiliated order branches founded in the East Riding. This material has been used to determine when and where the various affiliated orders first appear in the county, their place of origin, and their subsequent spread from community to community. It is thus possible to chart the progress of a major social movement and to suggest methods of dissemination.

The information on date of founding and the yearly details of membership and funds available from branch records, order directories and the returns made to the Registrar of Friendly Societies contributes valuable statistics on the fluctuations in the fortunes of the movement. Despite limited corroboratory evidence the initial explosion in the years 1838-43 would seem to be linked with the implementation of the New Poor Law and the major down-swing in 1848-52 appears to be both part of the general collapse of working-class movements in mid-century and a reflection of the crisis in agriculture. Later swings also coincide with fluctuations in agricultural wages and prices.

All recent writers who have dealt with friendly societies have commented on the elusiveness of information on the social and occupational status of the membership. Historians may differ on the subject of the total number of friendly society members at any one time, with opinions varying from less than a third to around half of the adult males in Great Britain, but with such totals there is no doubt that the membership did include a considerable portion of the lower working class. The great success of the affiliated orders in rural areas where the bulk of the population would come in this category belies the typical view as expressed in 1909 by the actuary Brabrook to the Royal Commission on the Poor Law that the membership of friendly societies represented 'very fairly the aristocracy of the wage earning classes' with very limited numbers of unskilled and agricultural labourers.[24] Such an opinion is not supported by the detailed information that is readily available in the proposition and membership books of affiliated branches and the following study corrects previous views on the social composition of rural societies which have been largely based on the contemporary impressions of actuaries and urban based commentators.

In the studies made of rural societies the principal sources have been local newspapers and it is their descriptions of feast days that have led to numerous accounts of upper class dominance and deferential membership of village clubs. Such a picture is challenged in this study by information gleaned on the management of affiliated branches from minute books and details on the social composition of leadership. The presence of the upper classes at friendly society feasts at the end of the nineteenth century and early twentieth century is revealed as not reflecting the subservience of village clubs but instead showing their political importance in the wake of the 1884 Reform Act. This is a theme that should be further developed.

There is scope for a much more detailed analysis of certain of the records than has been undertaken in this study. The prime role of the societies in providing benefits in sickness and on death is given only limited attention here but, as demonstrated, the information in the subscription, sickness and cash books of individual societies allows for a re-assessment of the financial value of friendly society membership. The membership books of certain societies by giving the addresses of members annually are similarly a source of exciting new material on working-class mobility in Victorian England.

The number of local and regional studies of friendly societies is increasing but until a great deal more work is done on the original records of both urban and rural affiliated order branches a definitive account of what was clearly the most successful working-class organisation in Victorian Britain cannot be written.[25] It is vital that the records of individual branches and districts, which are daily being destroyed, are located and deposited in record offices.

1

The Rural East Riding: The Victorian Background

The East Riding provides an ideal unit for study. Except for a few miles it is bounded on all sides by water with the rivers Ouse and Derwent and the Humber estuary marking the western, northern and southern boundaries and the North Sea the eastern. Although each of the three main natural regions, Holderness, the Wolds and the Vale of York display individual characteristics the overwhelming agricultural nature of the county gives it a homogeneity not present in many other similarly extensive administrative areas.

In 1840 the principal towns were Hull, Beverley, Bridlington and Driffield. Hull, with a population rising from 32,958 in 1831 to 275,486 in 1911, dominated the surrounding area but it was, as a trading and fishing port, more concerned with the wider world than with its agricultural hinterland. It was administratively outside the East Riding and therefore is not considered directly in this study. Beverley, the county town, was a minor industrial centre with tanning, shipbuilding and the manufacture of agricultural machinery providing the bulk of employment. Driffield in the mid-nineteenth century developed as an agricultural processing centre and Bridlington as a resort. There were also a number of small market towns with fewer than 2,500 inhabitants: Howden, Pocklington, Market Weighton, Hornsea, Hedon and Patrington. By the 1860s there could be added to these old established urban areas the growing resorts of Filey and Withernsea and the suburban settlements of Cottingham, near Hull,

Norton, near Malton, and Fulford, near York. Towns in the North and West Ridings which influenced areas of the East Riding because they were marketing or administrative centres were York, Malton, Scarborough, Selby and Goole.[1]

In the early nineteenth century a network of turnpike or other improved roads linked the main towns of the county but many areas were isolated by the river systems. There were few bridges across the rivers and until the opening of the first railway line in the East Riding, from Selby to Hull, in 1840 much of the commercial traffic within, and to and from, the county was by the various rivers and the navigable waterways. A whole series of railway lines opened up the county in the mid-nineteenth century.[2]

By 1850 the Wolds was the leading farming area of the county. Here large arable farms ranging from 300-1300 acres predominated and the farmsteads were often at a distance from the village. The standard of farming in much of the lowland regions of Holderness and the Vale of York, where there were many small family-run farms often of less than fifty acres, was considered backward by contemporaries. Southern Holderness however was far more prosperous and progressive and here large arable farms from 200-800 acres in extent were to be found. The majority of the larger farmers in the county were tenants of landed estates.[3]

The East Riding was dominated by large estates and in 1873 sixty per cent of its 700,000 acres of farmland were in the hands of only ninety-three owners each holding over 1000 acres. Eleven of these landowners had over 10,000 acres each and between them owned twenty-eight per cent of the land.[4] Some of the great owners were resident, such as Sir Tatton Sykes at Sledmere with 30,000 acres and Lord Wenlock at Escrick with 20,000 acres, but many were non-resident or made infrequent and short visits to their estates.[5]

With comparatively few resident gentry the leading figures in the countryside tended to be the clergy and large tenant farmers, and the doctors, solicitors and leading tradesmen of the market towns. The Anglican clergy often found themselves as the only representatives of the 'influential classes' resident in the villages. But their influence was limited by 'the apathy of the lower orders', the indifference of the landowners and farmers and above all by the prevalence of Dissent. At Foston in 1865 the vicar stated that 'The whole of the people may be said to be Dissenters or at any event not church in principle or practice' and at Acklam the disconsolate curate claimed that 'almost every individual in the parish leans to, or supports, Dissent . . . out of a population of 800 I should think there were not 20 real churchmen'.[6] In 1865 the rector of Catwick analysed the religious persuasion of his flock as follows:

> Houses in parish 55. Inhabited by Churchmen 18, Wesleyans 13, Primitive Methodists 14. Uncertain 10 but with leanings more to sect than to Church . . . Population of parish 270 - the greater part of whom - the labouring class - are as a rule Primitive Methodists. The class just above them such as the village shop keeper - blacksmith, or smaller tenant of land Wesleyans - and the upper class of farmers (and alas! the indifferent or such as have had a quarrel with one or other sect) churchmen.[7]

The returns of the Census of Religious Worship of 1851 confirm the strength of Methodism in the East Riding in the mid-nineteenth century. Only Cornwall of all the English counties had higher attendances at Methodist places of worship.[8] The support for the more 'radical' Primitive Methodism was particularly marked.[9] If the extent of Methodism was one of the particular characteristics of the Victorian East Riding another was the distinctive nature of its agricultural workforce.

The agricultural workforce of the East Riding consisted of three main groups; agricultural labourers who were hired by the day or week and usually lived in cottage accommodation in the village; farm servants who were hired by the year and lived in on the farm; and family labour provided by the farmers and their resident male relatives. In 1851 agricultural labourers formed forty-three per cent of the total labour force, farm servants thirty-three per cent and family labour twenty-four per cent. Family labour was particularly important on the small farms of the Vale of York while farm servants and agricultural labourers predominated on the large farms of the Wolds and parts of Holderness.[10] What was distinctive about the East Riding's workforce was the extent of the annual Martinmas hirings of the young unmarried male and female servants and their living-in on the farm. Statistics compiled by Dunbabin from the census returns show that in 1851 only two counties, Cumberland and Westmorland, had a higher proportion of 'indoor' to 'outdoor' farm servants than the East Riding.[11]

Generally the continuation in the later nineteenth century of hirings and living-in is considered a feature of the small farms in the northern pastoral counties but in the East Riding it was linked to the large arable farms of the Wolds and south Holderness.[12] The living-in by young men in isolated farmhouses and the custom whereby the great majority changed their workplace each year created a more mobile and independent minded rural working class than was common in much of England. The farm-servants' independent attitude was much criticised by clergy and farmers.[13]

The common portrayal of the hirings-fair as a riotous festive event loses sight of its significance as an occasion of collective bargaining on the part of the farm servant. The hirings allowed a man to choose his master as much as a master to choose his servant. When there was scarcity of labour and abundance of work the farm servant had the upper hand at the hirings and after.[14] Dunbabin has shown, as contemporaries suggested, that in those areas where the hirings and living-in persisted there was little support for agricultural worker trade unions.[15] The farm servants felt they had no need for unions as they bargained themselves for increased wages each year, often with success and it was difficult to unionise the workers on the large isolated farms. The farm labourers of the East Riding were also reluctant to combine and this can be partly attributed to the fact that they were paid considerably more than their counterparts in the south and that they could obtain more regular employment. In 1848 Legard considered that the East Riding labourers were amongst the best-paid in England and although this position was gradually eroded they remained among the better paid up to the First World War.[16]

The weakness of the support for agricultural trade unions in the East Riding in the 1870s echoed the limited discontent in the county during the Captain Swing movement of 1830-32.[17] But this passivity on the part of the East Riding farm worker and seeming lack of radicalism was not a sign of deference and dependence. The East Riding farm worker was no more a deferential traditionalist than the farm servant of North-East Scotland whom Ian Carter has championed.[18]

The distinctive elements of East Riding rural society in the nineteenth century were the overwhelming support for Methodism and the continuation and development of the tradition that the young men would spend the first ten years of their working life as hired farm servants. Neither of these two elements contributed to producing a dependent, submissive, cap touching proletariat. In Methodism, particularly Primitive Methodism, the labourers and rural artisans demonstrated their independence from the control of clergy and landowner and in the hirings and mutualism of living-in were learnt the benefits of collective action. This independence and collective action were combined in the village branches of the affiliated order friendly societies to produce what was the only strong rural working-class organisation in the Victorian countryside.

2

The Arrival and Spread of the Affiliated Orders in the East Riding

Friendly societies are of two main types, local societies and affiliated societies. The former are autonomous village or town benefit clubs while the latter are branches of national affiliated order friendly societies such as the Independent Order of Oddfellows, the Ancient Order of Foresters, and the Loyal Order of Ancient Shepherds. This study is primarily concerned with affiliated societies.

The first known local society in the East Riding was opened at Howden in 1751 and between then and 1830 at least forty-four friendly societies were established in twenty-seven towns and villages in the county. Half these societies were opened in market towns and only a handful in purely agricultural settlements.[1] By the early 1830s many of the local societies had either closed or were clearly in decline. During 1830-32 over twenty friendly societies were broken-up including the Beverley Brotherly Society founded in 1776, the Beverley New Friendly Society founded 1789, and the Market Weighton Friendly Society founded 1794.[2] An ageing membership and the difficult economic situation in 1828-30 were the chief factors that brought about the downfall of so many societies. The hardships faced at this time by the rural community in the East Riding were not as great as in the 'low-wage' counties of the south and west of England but prolonged unemployment, considerable emigration and widespread unrest were experienced.[3] A Driffield clergyman commented in the spring of 1830 that 'Poverty was the complaint of all ranks and degrees'.[4] Agricultural wages and prices improved in 1832 and local savings banks had record takings.[5] There was a similar revival of interest in friendly societies. In the years 1833-6 thirteen new societies were opened in the East Riding, more than the number of new societies recorded in the previous twenty-five years. All the new societies, however, were branches of either the Independent Order of Oddfellows, Manchester Unity or the Ancient Order of Foresters and it was the affiliated orders that rapidly filled the vacuum created by the decline of the local societies at a time when working men were clearly looking for ways to provide for themselves under the threat of the 'bastilles' of the New Poor Law.

The majority of the affiliated orders had their origins in the industrial areas of Lancashire and the West Riding and it was from the west that they entered the East Riding.[6] A pattern developed with the initial establishment of branches, known as 'lodges' by the Oddfellows and 'courts' by the Foresters, in the towns then spreading out into the surrounding countryside. The first order to appear in the county was the Independent Order of Oddfellows, Manchester Unity (100F MU) which had already opened a lodge at Hull by 1827. In 1831 the Wellington lodge at Howden was opened, then followed lodges in the towns of Beverley, 1832, Market Weighton and Great Driffield in 1833, Pocklington 1834 and Bridlington 1836.

From these centres the order successfully missioned the surrounding area so that by 1843 fifty-five Oddfellows lodges had been opened in the county thirty-nine of them in villages.[7] A similar pattern of development occurred in the case of the Ancient Order of Foresters (AOF). Its first court was established at Howden in 1836 by a court from Goole which in turn had been opened by a Doncaster court the year before. The order then spread out from Howden during the next two years to Newport, Holme upon Spalding Moor and Market Weighton. In 1838-9 thirty courts were opened including ones at the towns of Pocklington, Driffield, Bridlington, Beverley, Patrington and twenty-three villages.[8] There was great rivalry to open new courts and seemingly no central control. Hull courts were particularly active in South Holderness and the villages to the north and west of the town. During one week in July 1838 two courts were opened, with much celebration, at Cottingham, one by the officers of Court Kingston and the other by Court Foresters' Home. Court Kingston headed the Hull and East Riding District while Court

Foresters' Home headed the rival Hull and Lindsey District.[9] The battle for control of the area was only resolved on the latter court's secession to the Royal Order of Foresters in 1841.[10] By the end of 1844 forty-eight AOF courts had been opened in the East Riding.[11]

The Shepherds, Druids and Gardeners arrived in the wake of the Oddfellows and Foresters and had their greatest following in the north and west of the county. In 1837-8 the Leeds district of the Loyal Order of Ancient Shepherds opened lodges at Malton, Beverley and Hull and these three lodges were directly responsible for opening a further twenty-seven lodges in the East Riding between September 1838 and November 1846.[12] Thirteen of the lodges were founded from Malton the opening of one of which, at Wetwang in January 1839, was described as follows in the *Yorkshire Gazette*:

> On Monday week last, a deputation from the Shepherd's lodges in the Malton district, belonging to New and Old Malton, proceeded to the village of Wetwang, near Driffield to open a new lodge of the loyal order of Shepherds in that village. The new lodge is called 'The Shepherd's Delight' and is held at the house of Mr. Wm. Shields, the Black Swan Inn. On the occasion in question, 18 young men were initiated into the arcana and mysteries of the order after which they, along with the deputies, sat down to a most excellent and substantial dinner, amply provided for them in true Shepherds' hospitality by the worthy host, and to which ample justice was done. In the course of the day, the deputies and the newly made members perambulated the village, attended by a good band of music, and created such a sensation as had never before been known in the retired village of Wetwang. We understand the order meets with much encouragement and success, and is rapidly increasing in this neighbourhood.[13]

It was from the Malton area also that three of the four lodges of the Ancient Free Gardeners, opened in the East Riding in 1838-9, were founded.[14] Similarly the seven 'gorsedds' of the Loyal Order of Druids opened in the county in 1839-43 were promoted from the north, on this occasion from Scarborough.[15] The temperance Independent Order of Rechabites which had strong links with Nonconformity was the only other order to make any impact in the East Riding in this period and eight Rechabite tents were opened 1838-43 all in towns with the exception of Skipsea and North Cave.[16]

Table 1: Foundation Dates of East Riding Local and Affiliated Friendly Societies 1820-49

Year	No. founded	Year	No. founded
1820	0	1835	3
1821	1	1836	8
1822	0	1837	9
1823	0	1838	36
1824	3	1839	38
1825	0	1840	17
1826	0	1841	13
1827	0	1842	17
1828	2	1843	9
1829	0	1844	4
1830	0	1845	0
1831	1	1846	5
1832	1	1847	0
1833	4	1848	1
1834	2	1849	0

Source: Neave, thesis, Appendix 1.

Table 1 shows clearly that the years 1836-43 were the boom period for friendly society establishment and that is when the affiliated orders made their greatest impact in the East Riding. Of the 147 societies established in these years 143 were branches of the orders and only four were local societies. This explosion, which reached its peak in the period June 1838-June 1839 when some sixty branches were opened in the East Riding, also occurred throughout Lancashire and Yorkshire and came at a period of heady working-class activity in the industrial north with Chartism and the Anti-Poor Law campaigns.[17] The severe unemployment, industrial distress, and sharp rises in domestic prices of the years 1837-42 which activated these socio-political movements would not seem to be conducive to the establishment of organisations which required regular financial contributions and periodic expenditure on drinking, feasting and regalia. However in this period 'the want of trade and the demand for labour', which later on was seen as having an adverse effect on the prosperity of the affiliated orders, did not hinder their initial expansion.[18] Conversely the incentive for expansion would appear to have come out of economic distress and also from concern about the New Poor Law of 1834.

The Poor Law Amendment Act was passed in the middle of August 1834 and in the following months the poor were urged by the press to seek, in friendly society membership, a refuge from the evils of the workhouse and the ending of outdoor relief.[19] That large numbers did immediately seek such refuge was shown the following year in a report to the Poor Law Commissioners from the Registrar of Friendly Societies, Tidd Pratt, which recorded a marked increase in the number of benefit societies and savings bank deposits since the passing of the act. He confidently attributed the doubling of friendly society registrations to the workings of the act and three years later he reported that his conclusions on the links between the act and the expansion of friendly societies was borne out by conversations and correspondence with founder members.[20]

Others were similarly convinced that the expansion of the orders was directly linked to the implementation of the New Poor Law. A correspondent to the *Hull Advertiser* in March 1839, writing about the spread of the Ancient Order of Foresters in the area gave his opinion that:

> The present poor laws, no doubt, act as a stimulus in the formation of societies of this description . . . The increase in the members of this society appears from the opening of unions throughout the kingdom to be very great.[21]

Charles Hardwick, a leading Oddfellow and a great publicist of the order and friendly societies in general, expressed the view in 1859 that 'the true origin and rapid growth among the sound-hearted British populace of sick clubs and other friendly societies' was 'the honourable substitute for the parish relief of the semi-slave by act of Parliament'.[22]

Evidence from the East Riding lends support to these

somewhat biased contemporary views. It is noticeable that it was not until after the implementation of the Act in the East Riding at the end of 1836 that the explosion in friendly society provision occurred. The Beverley, Bridlington, Driffield and Pocklington Guardians held their first meetings in October-November 1836, and the Howden Guardians in February 1837.[23] In particular the peak period coincided with the enlargement or opening of new workhouses. New workhouses were opened at Driffield and Patrington in 1838, Skirlaugh and Howden in 1839 and Sculcoates and Selby in 1842.[24] Only three friendly societies were founded in Driffield Poor Law Union area in the eighteen months between the establishment of the Union and the opening of the workhouse but at least sixteen were founded in the following twelve months.[25]

Boards of Guardians were actively encouraged by the Commissioners to promote friendly societies and in January 1837 they issued an 'Instructional letter addressed to various Boards of Guardians on their formation' in which it was stated that:

> the Commissioners trust that you will, each in his own neighbourhood do all in your power to promote the formation of such habits of forethought, of frugality, and self-dependence, as will keep them the able-bodied poor from falling back into pauperism, by aiding the establishment of sick-clubs, savings banks, and annuity societies; and by inculcating on your labourers and servants the importance of thus guarding against loss of work, sickness, and old age . . .[26]

Certain East Riding guardians did openly support friendly societies in their areas. Henry Grimston of Kilnwick on the Wolds, the chairman of Driffield Guardians, seemingly reserved his support for the large Etton Amicable and Friendly Society which had been founded by his father, but his vice-chairman, the Revd John Blanchard, was particularly active in the promotion of the affiliated orders.[27] Blanchard was a magistrate and the patron and rector of the wealthy living of Middleton on the Wolds where he owned 900 acres and lived in a large Georgian mansion. He was by far the largest landowner in his parish and with his sporting interests was a typical Victorian 'squarson'. In 1833 he had gained great notoriety by imprisoning the farm labourer Jeremiah Dodsworth for non-payment of tithes on his wages.[28] Blanchard would seem an unlikely figure to become closely involved with the affiliated orders but he was to become a popular preacher at anniversary services and was often the chairman at society feasts. He was an annual subscriber to Middleton and Lockington Foresters and Lund Oddfellows from their establishment in 1839-40.[29] In his sermon at the anniversary of Court Rose of the Dale, Ancient Order of Foresters, at Kilham in 1842, he was said to have expressed great disquiet at some of the provisions of the New Poor Law.[30]

Both the first chairman and vice-chairman of Howden Board of Guardians, Thomas Clarke and the Revd Thomas Guy were patrons of the town's old established Union and Friendly Societies as well as actively supporting Oddfellows' lodges in the area.[31] Clarke was proud of his 'spacious Union Workhouse' which he described as 'a pleasing, cheerful and ornamental structure'. He was full of praise for the New Poor Law which he thought brought great benefits to the poor who were 'not only much more considerably cared for, . . . their comforts have increased, and what is best of all there is an increased and improved spirit of independence and self-reliance and by consequence greater efficiency and extended happiness and content.'[32]

The circular sent out by the Poor Law Commissioners in April 1840 which laid down that friendly society members should not receive relief from their societies and the poor rates simultaneously may have been a factor in slowing down the expansion of the orders from that year but it is more likely this was caused by the over abundance of societies already opened and the worsening economic situation for both the agricultural and industrial labourer from late 1841.[33] The distress of the winter of 1841-2 saw the first substantial draw on the funds of many of the new societies. In February 1842 the two lodges of the 100F MU in Market Weighton granted sums of from £1 to £3 to members who were unemployed and the Beverley district of the order was paying out travelling allowances of 18d a time to as many as twenty members a day.[34] The *Hull Advertiser* commented:

> This great demand is necessarily materially diminishing funds set apart for that purpose and if not

> speedily averted may be productive of serious consequences to the welfare of the societies.[35]

A number of societies did fail at this time and at least seventeen East Riding affiliated branches had closed by 1845. The boom period of the orders was over.

3

Fluctuating Fortunes

A 'smash amongst the Secret Orders' 1848-52

The affiliated orders, nationally and locally, lost ground in the late 1840s-early 1850s. Individual courts and lodges collapsed because of declining membership and lack of funds, and many branches were expelled, seceded or were voluntarily closed owing to the great internal disruptions that beset the chief orders in the period. Prosperous districts and branches began to question the authority and actions of the national committees and officers and secessions occurred in the face of what the rebels considered an excessive centralisation of management.[1]

The reversal of fortune for the IOOF MU began in 1844 when the Annual Committee passed two resolutions which eroded the independence of the lodges. Delegates to the Annual Committee were to be from districts instead of from each lodge, as formerly, and the lodges were to be compelled to send in a statement of their financial positions to the Board of Directors. This last proposal was with a view to an investigation into the condition of the order, and the adoption of necessary reforms. Lodges hitherto had the right to fix their own rates of contributions and benefits and so the mere prospect of any interference with this right produced great agitation.[2] Three districts, 123 lodges and 15,840 members were suspended for refusing to make returns. When at the 1845 Annual Committee further resolutions were passed that forced upon the lodges certain

Table 2: National Membership of Four Affiliated Orders 1846-60

Year	IOOF MU	AOF 1 Jan.	LOAS 1 Jan.	IOR April	Total
1846	259374	76990	14169	18268	368793
1848	249261	84472	15751	12500	361984
1850	224878	80089	14636	9060	328663
1852	225194	89875	14540	6733	336342
1854	232228	100556	17277	6005	356066
1856	251008	113752	18151	5940	388851
1858	276254	135001	18586	6009	435850
1860	305214	168576	23477	6115	503382

Sources: AOF/IOOF MU, F.G.P. Neison 'Some Statistics of the Affiliated Orders of Friendly Societies' *Journal of the Statistical Society*, March 1877, pp. 42-81;
LOAS, *Annual Reports*; D.H. Hague, *LOAS Historical Sketch*, n.d.;
IOR, R. Highet, *Rechabite History*, Manchester, 1936, p. 501.

financial improvements there occurred the crisis which culminated in what is termed the 'national split' and saw the formation of the National Independent Order of Odd Fellows.[3]

A similar split occurred in the Loyal Order of Ancient Shepherds, Ashton Unity. At the LOAS annual meeting in 1848 Wisbech district proposed that the law which fined any district for not sending its full representation to an annual meeting be rescinded. On this proposal being rejected the Wisbech and Cambridge districts, which had 10 per cent of the members of the order, seceded and founded the Wisbech Unity. The following year further proposals which challenged the supremacy of the Ashton district were also lost and so in 1850 a number of Yorkshire lodges and districts held a public meeting in York 'the object being to shake, if not to destroy, the Ashton Unity'. The order expelled the thirty-four ringleaders of the agitation, five of whom came from Hull district, the others from Leeds, Pontefract and Wakefield. As a result thirty-nine west Yorkshire lodges with 1579 members seceded.[4] In eastern Yorkshire in the years 1849-51 seventeen lodges left the order and 423 individual members were suspended or expelled.[5]

The AOF did not attempt to interfere with the independence of its courts at this period but actions of the High Court led to dissensions and secessions in 1848-9 and a reduction in membership. Certain courts in London District in 1848 questioned the authority of the High Court to decide on where it should invest the surplus funds of the order and the rebel courts formed a 'Protective Committee' and managed to have the money of the order locked up for fifteen months. Forty-three courts were suspended and thirty of the leaders were expelled. In 1849 a financial crisis in Liverpool district added to the disturbances and resulted in pressure on the courts for financial reforms.[6]

The collapse of the Independent Order of Rechabites occurred earlier than the reversals experienced by the other orders and its decline was the most prolonged. Membership had risen from 3200 in 1838 to a peak of 22,684 in 1844.[7] At the Annual Moveable Conference in July 1842 new scales of contributions for sickness and funeral benefits were introduced which resulted in the other being immediately 'violently convulsed in almost every part; opposition of a most decided character was manifested by both tents and districts'.[8] Amendments were made to the new financial regulations the next year but there was general disapproval when the moveable committee abolished the password and substituted cards of admission instead. To this unrest was added the attempt on the part of the order to obtain an act of enrolment, to protect its funds, in 1843 and the years following. This move was violently opposed by many tents and districts who saw the proposed bill as a 'bill of penalties, which would confine them to slavery; others thought that it would unalterably bind them to a certain line of conduct, destroying the then constitution of the Order.'[9] Few of the seventy-six districts of the order remained active after the enrolment crisis and the membership was reduced by 74 per cent in the years 1844-56.[10]

Except in the case of LOAS few East Riding affiliated branches were directly involved in these various disruptions but the general repercussions were clearly felt in the area. As Stead noted in his history of the affiliated orders: 'During times of contention and trouble many nervous and peaceable members lose confidence and withdraw themselves from the society they belong to'.[11] Table 3 below shows that in East Yorkshire all the orders discussed above experienced a marked fall in the number of branches in the late 1840s-early 1850s. The 125 branches of the Foresters, Oddfellows, Shepherds and Rechabites recorded as existing in 1845 had been more than halved by 1860.

Table 3: Affiliated Orders in East Yorkshire 1845-60

Order	Branches	Number existing in			
		1845	1850	1852	1860
A.O.F.*	48 by 1844	37	34	27	26
I.O.O.F. MU*	55 by 1843	49	36	n.a.	21
L.O.A.S.**	40 by 1843	33	30	20	14
I.O.R.*	7 by 1844	6	2	n.a.	1
Total	150	125	102		62

* East Riding
** Malton District (3 sub-districts in East Riding, 3 in N. Riding)
Sources: AOF, *Directory*, 1845, 1850, 1852, 1860;
IOOF, *List of Lodges*, 1845, 1850, 1860;
LOAS, *Annual Reports*, 1843, 1845, 1850, 1852, 1860;
IOR, *HMC Reports*, 1840-1, 1844, 1851, 1861.

The exact timing of the closures is difficult to determine but at least twenty-two East Riding societies were dissolved in the years 1844-53 with peaks of six closures in 1848 and seven in 1850.[12] In the early summer of 1848 the *Hull Advertiser* reported the dissolution of Oddfellows clubs at Bridlington, Flamborough, Hunmanby, Skipsea and Wetwang. The failure of the last was attributed to 'losses occasioned by the refusal of members to repay loans advanced them, and from other causes'.[13] Also in 1848 the Foresters' court closed at Hedon and in 1850 a Foresters' court and an Oddfellows' lodge at Cottingham, a Shepherds' lodge at Yeddingham and four branches of affiliated orders at Driffield were 'broken-up'.[14]

Fuller details are available on the declining fortunes of the societies in the market town of Great Driffield. In 1848, Driffield, an important agricultural marketing, processing and supply centre, had a population approaching 4000. The town had expanded rapidly in the previous fifteen years with some 266 buildings being erected including 180 cottages, forty-seven houses, twenty-seven shops, three public houses, two steam flour mills, a brewery, a corn exchange, an iron manufactory and a bone mill.[15] The comparatively youthful and prosperous working population provided fertile ground for the affiliated orders and at least eight branches of orders were established in Driffield by 1843 and it is likely that a larger number of short-lived societies, dividing and burial clubs, existed alongside them in over twenty public houses and half-a-dozen beerhouses.[16]

There were already two thriving local societies in the town in the 1830s: the Union Friendly Society, founded 1793, with 389 members in 1840, and the Driffield Provident Society founded in 1823 which had eighty-one members in 1844.[17] To these were added two lodges of the Independent Order of Oddfellows, Manchester Unity in 1833 and 1838; three courts of the Ancient Order of Foresters, in 1838, 1840 and 1842; a tent of the Independent Order of Rechabites in 1839; a lodge of the Loyal Order of Ancient Shepherds, Ashton Unity in 1840 and a gorsedd of the Ancient Order of Druids in 1843.[18] Only one of these ten societies, the two local and the eight affiliated societies, was still functioning after 1870. Some had a particularly short existence and of one of them, Court Diana AOF, we only know that it opened in 1840 and had either closed or left the order by 1845. The great collapse of the affiliated orders in Driffield took place in 1850 and surprisingly it was the older established Oddfellows' lodges which broke up first.

The *Hull Advertiser* of 12 April 1850 announced the dissolution of the Rising Sun Lodge and on 24 May following reported that:

> The whole of the regalia of the defunct 'Loyal Rising Sun' Lodge of Odd Fellows, in Driffield, was sold by auction on Tuesday last, the very day on which just seventeen years ago it was founded with great *eclat* and bright hopes of its future prospects.[19]

Less than a month later on 14 June the same paper reported under the heading - **Driffield - Smash Amongst The Secret Orders** - that:

> These societies, of which so much was said of their boasted ability, are being fast scattered to the winds. The breaking up of the 'Rising Sun' Lodge of Odd Fellows and the sale of the regalia has been quickly followed by the dissolution of the 'Coronation' Lodge

> of the same order, and the 'Fold of Refuge' Lodge of the order of Ancient Shepherds; the Foresters being the only club on the secret order system now left in Driffield.[20]

The surviving club was Court Alfred the Great, for the third Foresters' court, Court Olive Branch, also closed in 1850.[21] Two other affiliated order branches lasted a little longer for the Rechabite tent was not closed until 1863-5, and the Druids gorsedd still existed in 1864.[22]

When reporting the anniversaries of the Union and Provident societies in July 1850 the newspaper commented on their funds and membership figures that 'These statistics speak well for the old benefit societies, some of which are likely to long survive the secret orders'.[23] The following year they were said to be still 'weathering the storm', however along with the other Driffield societies they had undergone considerable reduction in membership in the period 1845-50.[24]

Table 4: Membership of Driffield Friendly Societies 1845-52

	1845	1850	1852
IOOF MU Rising Sun Lodge	155	121 *	-
IOOF MU Coronation Lodge	86	49 *	-
AOF Court Alfred the Great	103	64	62
AOF Court Olive Branch	9	6 *	-
Ancient Order of Druids	13 (1846)	13	8
Union Friendly Society	297 (1844)	177	141 (1853)
Provident Society	81 (1844)	69	67 (1851)
Total	744	499	

* closed 1850

Sources: AOF, *Directory*, 1845, 1850, 1852; IOOF, *List of Lodges*: 1845, 1850; *Hull Advertiser*, 12/7/44, 12/7/50, 18/7/51, 15/7/53; HCRO DDX 61/1.

The Provident Society continued to decline in the early 1850s and it too was dissolved in July 1854 when the remaining sixty-one members divided the funds of £1268 amongst themselves.[25] The old established Union Society which once had over 600 members suffered severely during the 1840s and 1850s and it never recovered. In 1840 it had 389 members and funds of £2291, by 1850 these figures had been reduced to 177 members and £1295 and in 1865 there were only sixty-four members and £715.[26] In a report of the anniversary in July 1845 it was noted that 'The society was at one time one of the most extensive and wealthiest benefit clubs in the neighbourhood; but, like most other societies founded on similar principles, it has been considerably reduced of late years, especially since the various orders became so popular'.[27] The majority of the members attending the anniversary in 1862 were said to be 'grey old men, many of them walking with the aid of a couple of sticks'.[28] The society was finally dissolved in 1870.[29]

The reversal in fortune experienced by the affiliated orders in mid-century deserves much closer attention for it coincided with similar setbacks to a variety of organisations concerned with religious, political, educational and financial advancement of the working class and it was a period which saw a crucial change of direction in the labour movement generally. Other organisations which depended on the support of the 'respectable' working classes, Mechanics Institutes, savings banks and Methodism, encountered such reversals both nationally and locally.

East Riding Mechanics' Institutes all experienced a decline in membership. At Beverley the Mechanics' Institute suffered a fall in membership from 342 at the end of 1848 to 191 in early 1855; at Driffield membership fell from 246 in 1849 to 180 in 1854, at Hedon from ninety in March 1848 to thirty in 1853; at Pocklington from 148 in 1850 to fifty-eight in 1852; and at Market Weighton from 130 in June 1848 to eighty-one in 1850.[30] The reasons for the decline in support for the Mechanics' Institutes are less obvious than in the case of savings banks and Methodism.

Reaction against the authoritarian rule of national officers and executives which led to schisms in the affiliated orders was also present in Methodism in mid-century. As a result of internal disputes in 1849 about 100,000 left the Wesleyan Methodists many forming themselves into a loosely organised body of 'Wesleyan Reformers'. This 'Reform' movement had only limited following in the East Riding but it made inroads into society membership in the Bridlington,

Table 5: Methodism and Savings Banks 1835-55

	Wesleyan and Primitive Change in membership	Methodism %	Savings Banks Increase in accounts	%
1835-45	+76562	+23	+516378	+94
1845-55	-63712	-16	+241979	+23

Sources: R. Currie, A. Gilbert and L. Horsley, *Churches and Churchgoers*, Oxford, 1977, pp. 140-1; H.O. Horne, *A History of Savings Banks*, London, 1947, pp. 386-7.

Beverley and Pocklington circuits in 1851-2. A close look at the quarterly returns for Beverley and Pocklington Circuits indicates that the decline in membership was most marked in the late summer and winter of 1851-2.[31] The Reform crisis largely accounts for the drop in membership but generally the average annual growth rates for both Wesleyan and Primitive Methodism were down during much of the period 1845-55. Currie records an average annual growth rate of -8.4 for Wesleyan Methodism for the triennial period 1851-3 and -0.9 for the next three years, the most severe set backs that beset the denomination during the nineteenth century.[32] Primitive Methodism, although benefiting by the upheavals in Wesleyanism in 1849-50, also recorded a slowing down or reversal in growth. Actual decreases in membership were recorded nationally in the years 1845-7 and 1853-5.[33] In the East Riding statistics from Driffield, Bridlington and Hornsea Primitive Methodist Circuits show membership being virtually stationary in 1850 then dropping in the summer-autumn of 1851 and remaining at a reduced figure until 1858-9.[34] The fall in support was both financial and numerical and accounts for the marked drop in the number of Methodist chapels built in the county. Only seven new chapels were opened in the five year period 1851-5, the previous and subsequent quinquennial totals being thirty-one and twenty-three.[35]

Savings banks which after twenty years of uninterrupted growth had actual overall decreases in their number of accounts and amount of deposits in 1847-8 were in further difficulties in 1849-50 following the panic fostered by the revelations of frauds by managers of banks in England and Ireland. In December 1849 it was discovered that the actuary of the Rochdale Savings Bank had swindled some £72,000.[36] With no guarantee of the funds by the state and no liability on the trustees the plight of the depositors was desperate. Confidence in savings banks was temporarily shattered and throughout the country investigations were made and numerous other frauds were revealed. In East Yorkshire frauds were uncovered early in 1850 at Hull, Scarborough and Market Weighton, while Beverley, Bridlington and Driffield Savings Banks were declared sound. The most serious case was at Market Weighton where it was discovered that the manager, a draper and influential Wesleyan Methodist class leader and trustee, had misappropriated nearly £2000.[37] The opinion which had long been held that savings banks 'can never involve those who there deposit their savings in any risk or expense' was found untrue and extensive withdrawals were made throughout the country.[38] The funds of Hull Savings Bank fell from £326,063 in 1845 to £278,994 in 1850.[39] Friendly societies, major depositors in savings banks, were understandably concerned and it is significant that in May 1850 Middleton Foresters decided to withdraw their funds out of Beverley Savings Bank and place them in Machell's Bank in the town.[40]

The disruptions experienced by the affiliated orders and Methodism and the distrust felt for savings banks were undoubtedly factors in the decline in support for these organisations in mid-century but of greater importance and of more immediate impact in the East Riding was the adverse state of the rural economy in the years 1848-52. In June 1849 George England, clerk to Howden Poor Law Union, wrote a letter to the Poor Law Commissioners commenting as follows on the problems then facing the local farming community:

> I beg to state that in my opinion the agriculturists in this district have cultivated their farms during the past year at considerable loss and that unless the next harvest should be a favourable one many of the occupiers must be placed in circumstances of pecuniary difficulties. There is at present a great scarcity of money amongst the farmers and several I have no doubt will be obliged to raise money by loan to pay the expenses of reaping their corn during the present year. Should the price of grain continue low it is impossible to foretell what the consequences in this

district may be.

> The funds of the savings bank here have during the last six months been reducing but not to any great extent. I believe part of the deposits have been withdrawn for the purpose of emigration but I have no doubt some of the sums withdrawn have been to meet the wants of the parties owing to the small sums realised from the last years crop. The time has not yet arrived to test the effect of the recent measures affecting the agricultural interest. It is not improbable but that next winter their operation in this district will be shewn by a scarcity of employment for the labouring poor and by an unwillingness on the part of the farmers to expend money except for work indispensable to carry on farming operations.[41]

The crisis for both the farmer and agricultural labourer was brought about by a combination of poor harvests and low prices. The four years of high prices which had assisted the expansion of the affiliated orders in the East Riding came to an end in the summer of 1842 when the price of wheat fell from 64*s* in June to 47*s* per quarter in December 1842. Good harvests in 1843 and 1844 helped to keep prices down, but an inadequate harvest in 1845 followed by a poor wheat harvest in both Britain and on the Continent in 1846 saw prices rise sharply in the autumn of 1846. Wheat prices reached a peak of 93*s* a quarter in June 1847. The following month a decline in prices began which continued with some minor fluctuations throughout 1848-52. The repeal of the Corn Laws which came into force in June 1846 did not seriously affect the price of corn until after March 1848, for in January 1847 the new Corn Laws had been suspended during the scarcity and high prices. The rise in imports following their reintroduction saw an almost uninterrupted decline in the price of wheat from 53*s* 11*d* in January 1848 to 36*s* 11*d* in May 1850, the lowest weekly average price since January 1836. This price was again reached in March 1851 and a rise in imports in autumn 1851 caused the price to fall further to only 35*s* 6*d* a quarter. The change to higher prices began in the second half of 1852.[42]

The price of corn was a major determining factor for the level of agricultural wages and continuity of employment in the East Riding. When the price of corn fell the farmer made savings by cutting his labour bill. Wages were reduced and the labourers' employment became intermittent. The drop in the prices of foodstuffs rarely offset the marked decline in income. An East Riding landowner, E.H. Reynard, of Sunderlandwick near Driffield, told a protectionist meeting in December 1849 that:

> He had inquired of his labourers whether they fared best when the price of corn was extremely low, or when it sold at a renumerative price to the grower, and they invariably answered that they found things were best with them when corn was at a fair price then they got most wages and could save most money.[43]

And seemingly also pay their subscriptions to a friendly society.

Figure 2 shows a marked correlation between the price of wheat and friendly society recruitment in the years 1843-55. When prices were at their lowest in 1850-1 recruitment was negligible but when the price of wheat reached a peak in 1855 new members poured into the societies.

Fig. 2 Wheat Prices and Affiliated Order Recruitment in the East Riding 1840-56

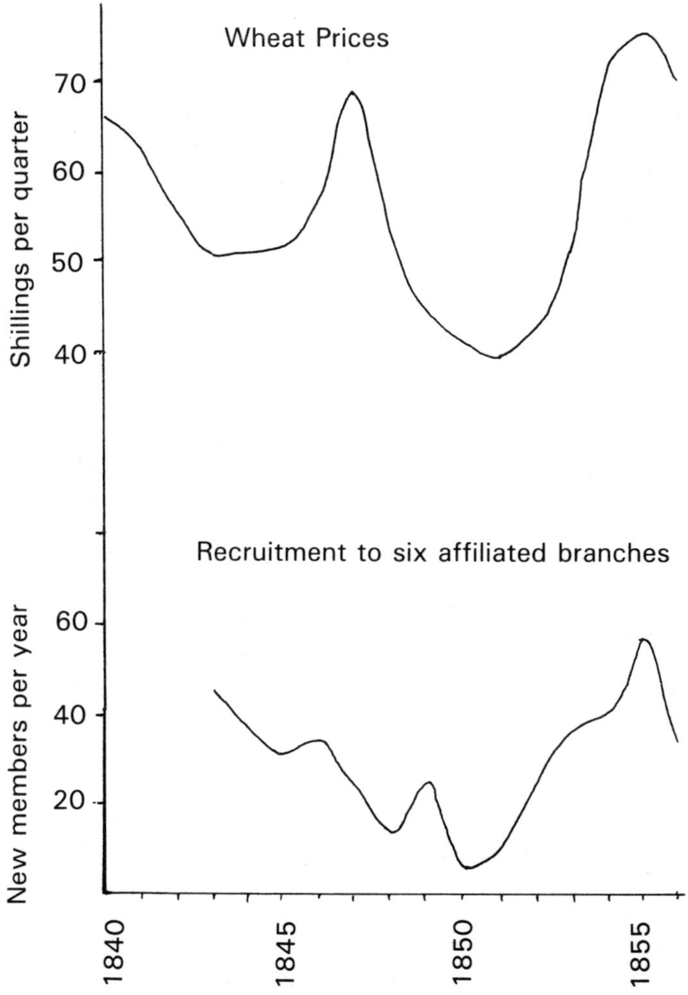

Sources: Wheat prices B.R. Mitchell and P. Deane, *Abstract of British Historical Statistics*, (Cambridge, 1971) pp. 488-9 Recruitment Proposition books Middleton AOF, Cranswick AOF, Lockington AOF, Hunmanby LOAS - Contribution books Lund IOOF, Ferriby IOOF.

Not only did recruitment to the societies drop in the years 1848-52 but so did overall membership. Figures available for nine East Riding affiliated branches show that all but one had less members in 1852 than four years earlier.[44] It is likely that this decline was due to the drop in recruitment coupled with a much higher number being excluded for non payment of subscriptions. In the case of Lund Oddfellows during the years 1848-52, when there were only eleven new recruits, twenty members were excluded for being in arrears, five withdrew on emigration, six transferred to other lodges and four died - a net loss of twenty-four. The number of members in arrears was particularly high at a time when the total membership of the lodge was only between fifty and seventy-five and it is no doubt an indication of the financial difficulties that rural labourers and farm servants were experiencing.[45]

No uninterrupted set of figures for agricultural labourers' wage rates in the East Riding has been found for this period but what limited information is available indicates a drop in wages in 1848-9, remaining low during 1850-2, followed by a marked rise in 1853-6.[46] A high proportion of the East Riding's agricultural workforce and new recruits to the friendly societies were not labourers but hired farm servants and therefore the annual fluctuations of their wages and their ability to obtain employment are highly significant. Newspaper reports of the Martinmas hirings in November 1849 record reductions in wages and many men being left unhired.[47] There was a large influx of servants to Driffield first hirings as very few had been engaged at the earlier hirings at Beverley and Sherburn. However the situation was little better at Driffield:

> From the present depressed state of the agricultural interest, and the greatest progress already made in field labour, owing to the favourable season, the farmers considered themselves in a position to expect a decrease of wages, and to dispense, for a time, with their usual number of hands. Owing to these circumstances, a comparatively less number of servants found masters than was usual in former years on similar occasions.[48]

After the later Martinmas week hirings at Driffield it was reported that 'Many of the middle class of agricultural servants remain unhired, and will probably continue so until after the depth of winter.'[49]

The weather in the early part of 1850 was particularly harsh and, with prices continuing low, unemployment was high. A speaker from Bishop Burton at a protectionist meeting at Beverley in February spoke of the hardships of the labourers. He claimed that they were not half-employed therefore half-price bread was of no benefit to them if no loaf could be purchased.[50] The local newspapers report the traditional signs of rural hardship and unrest; incendiarism, sheep stealing, poaching and above all emigration.[51]

Emigration fever hit the East Riding as elsewhere in the early 1850s. Nationally emigration rose sharply in 1847 and stayed high until 1855 with a peak in 1852.[52] Locally the greatest activity occurred in 1850-2: advertisements for emigrant ships and letters from local emigrants proliferated in the press; the latter usually echoing the sentiments expressed by a Driffield emigrant in Australia who wrote: 'A man has a chance to mend himself here, but he has none in England, - so farewell England'.[53] In one week in April 1850 four ships left Hull for America filled chiefly with agricultural labourers from Yorkshire and Lincolnshire.[54]

In 1852 the farming community saw their fortunes begin to change. In the Driffield area, where in 1851 the leading landlords Sykes and Langley had felt it necessary to return 10 per cent of their rents to the tenants, Lord Londesborough 'considerably advanced the rents of his farms and all the tenants still continue their holdings'.[55] Agricultural wages remained low until 1853 but fuller employment and low prices assisted the labourer and in reporting the success of the Driffield Savings Bank in 1852-3 an editorial in the *Driffield Observer* noted that 'The cheapness of bread and clothing has enabled hundreds of agricultural labourers and mechanics to save the means with which to improve their conditions'.[56] The ability to join, and confidence in, friendly societies and savings banks returned in 1852-3 and funds and recruitment to both rose markedly in the mid-1850s along with agricultural wages and wheat prices.

The farming boom and the second generation branches 1853-76

The recovery from the post-Repeal depression, which began

in the early months of 1853, was soon reflected in the figures for recruitment to the affiliated orders in the East Riding. The abundant harvest of 1854 and the good harvest of 1855 did not lead to low prices as was usual because the Crimean War greatly inflated the price of agricultural products.[57] During the war period March 1854 - April 1856 wheat prices rose to their highest point since 1818-19 reaching 78*s* a quarter in 1855 and 67*s* in 1856 on the Hull Corn Market and agricultural labourers' wages were raised.[58] Recruitment to friendly societies was particularly high in 1855 and Keyingham Foresters' court initiated seventy-seven new members, the average for the previous sixteen years being only ten. Membership was increased in that year by over 60 per cent and during the following eight years the court had an average of thirty-one initiations a year.[59] Confidence in the affiliated orders had clearly returned for although corn prices and wages began to drop in 1857 there was no comparable fall in support for friendly societies. The rural working class benefited from fuller employment for a decade from the mid 1850s and this was reflected in their willingness and ability to join and found affiliated branches.

The late 1850s saw the second major period of friendly society establishment in the East Riding and between 1856 and 1870 at least sixty-three new societies were opened. Over half of these societies belonged to four affiliated orders which made their first real impact in the county in these years. Six branches of the Independent Order of Oddfellows, Kingston Unity were opened 1856-63, eight branches of the United Ancient Order of Druids 1859-63, eleven branches of the Grand United Order of Oddfellows 1861-70, and eight branches of the National United Order of Free Gardeners 1868-70. The older established orders also opened some branches IOOF MU two in 1861, AOF three in 1858-65, and LOAS four in 1858-69.[60] This expansion of second generation affiliated branches owed much to a reluctance on the part of the labourer and artisan to join those societies founded twenty or thirty years before which now contained an increasing number of older members who were likely to draw heavily on the funds. The 'new' orders showed great missionary zeal and benefitted from the renewed confidence in friendly societies and the increased ability on the part of prospective members to subscribe.

The chief periods of friendly society establishment were 1861-5, thirty new societies, and 1869-70, sixteen. The period with least activity was 1866-8 with only seven new societies at which time there was a serious but temporary set back to the farming boom brought about by the rinderpest outbreak of 1865-7 which caused the loss of about 10 per cent of the East Riding's cattle population. This led farmers to cut back both wages and their labour force.[61] There was a widespread outbreak of incendiarism on the Wolds and in Holderness with reports beginning in September 1865 and continuing through the winter.[62] These years also saw a decline in recruitment, particularly in 1866, and a reduction in membership for some societies. The total membership of Lund Oddfellows fell from 155 in December 1863 to 134 in December 1866. During the period sixteen new members were initiated but twenty-nine were excluded for being in arrears.[63] The annual average intake of Keyingham Foresters in the years 1865-7 was only eleven, half the annual average for the decade 1861-70.[64] Middleton Foresters had 129 members in February 1863 and 131 in August 1869 yet during this period forty-nine joined. The net loss is largely accounted for by exclusions for arrears in payments. This society also had a drop in its funds in 1866.[65]

A further period of hardship was experienced by rural workers in 1871-2 when greatly increased prices of all foodstuffs led 'family after family' to fall by degrees into debt and difficulty.[66] Recruitment to East Riding friendly societies dropped in 1871-2 and membership levelled-off, no new societies were founded in 1871, [the first time since 1855], and there was a greater spate of friendly society closures in the first half of the 1870s than at any time since the early 1850s.[67] Only three new members joined Keyingham Foresters in 1872, the lowest number since 1844 and a great contrast to the annual average of seventeen for the period 1860-79.[68] Methodism, that other indicator of rural working-class activity, also showed a decline. Few new Methodist chapels were built in the early 1870s and there was an actual drop in membership in the Driffield Primitive Methodist Circuit in 1871-2.[69]

The major economic upswing of the early 1870s and the consequent urban movements for higher wages and shorter hours encouraged a limited growth of unionism amongst farm workers in 1871-3. In 1872-3 there was considerable trade union activity in the East Riding, strikes and union meetings being held at many places on the Wolds and in Holderness. A branch of the Agricultural Labourers'

Protection Society was founded at Kilham in February 1872; this later joined the Amalgamated Labour League which had an organising agent at Kilham by January 1873 and branches at Hull and Driffield.[70] Other labour clubs were founded at Bridlington and Hedon. Although there was plenty of agitation in the county and concern expressed in the press, the agricultural workforce of the East Riding, having a large element of farm servants, could not be successfully unionised. However the demands for higher wages were generally met by the farmers and in each district wages rose in the first half of the 1870s. Wage rises were particularly noticeable on the Wolds where servants obtained an increase of from £1 to £2 a year at the 1872 hirings.[71]

The higher wages obtained through the labourers' movement and the tightening of the labour market in some areas led to a temporary rise in recruitment and membership of friendly societies in 1875-7, just before the onset of the first wave of the agricultural depression of the last quarter of the century.[72]

Agricultural depression, rural decline and the coming of National Insurance 1875-1912

The forty years before the First World War are traditionally portrayed as a time of increasing difficulties for friendly societies. Numerically there was a substantial increase in overall membership but the actual and the projected claims on the funds of individual branches brought about by an ageing membership foretold widespread insolvency. Competition for subscribers from collecting societies, trade unions and commercial life assurance companies prevented any increase in contributions to alleviate the burden. The affiliated orders felt threatened also by the pressure for, and introduction of, contributory and non-contributory state schemes for old-age and sickness benefits.[73] In addition for rural societies there were the problems brought about by the long-lasting agricultural depression and marked decline in rural population.

In the East Riding one might have expected many friendly societies to have gone bankrupt under the strains of the last quarter of the century; however a surprising number emerged with increased membership and funds by 1900. Large affiliated branches understandably were the most resilient and out of the ten societies known to have closed in 1875-1900 six were old established local societies. The Etton Amicable and Friendly Society, once the largest society in the county, closed in 1876 after an existence of eighty-seven years, its membership and funds having been in decline since the 1830s and the arrival of the affiliated orders. The Wansford Provident Society founded 1792, closed soon after 1875; Etton female society founded 1841, dissolved 1880; Flamborough Fishermans' Fund founded 1809, was broken up by 1887; Newport Benefit Society founded 1824, dissolved 1887; Hedon Union Society founded 1799, dissolved 1897.[74] The fall in membership and funds of the last two in the 1870s and 1880s demonstrates the problems faced by such local societies. The Newport society had a membership of 200 and funds of £331 in 1880 but when it was dissolved seven years later these had been reduced to forty-seven and £80 respectively.[75] The Hedon society with 139 members and £1239 in 1872 had only fifty-seven members and £271 twenty-five years later. The bulk of the membership of these societies was elderly, seventy per cent of the members at the dissolution of the Hedon society in 1897 had belonged for over thirty years and only seven per cent had joined in the last ten years.[76]

Increasing longevity, which was greater among friendly society members than the population as a whole, and a dramatic rise in sickness claims by those over forty combined to erode the funds. For the affiliated orders generally it was the prospect of insolvency rather than declining membership that was the problem at the end of the century. There was however a drop in recruitment and a subsequent fall in membership for most branches during the worst years of the agricultural depression. The depression in arable farming in the county began in 1876 when a wet autumn in 1875 was followed by heavy rainfall in the winter of 1876-7 and then in the spring of 1878 began a period of two and a half years of exceptionally cold and wet weather. The 'disaster' of 1879 was followed by five years of exhaustion and recovery 1880-5.[77] Agricultural wages which had still been increasing in 1875-6 came under attack from farmers in 1877-8 and many farm servants found themselves unemployed in the winter months 1876-7 and 1877-8. In 1878 farmers cut wages by the high figure of between £2 and £5 per annum, and the fall in wages continued in 1879-80 and remained at a lower level throughout the

1880s.[78] Recruitment to the East Riding societies dropped in 1878, was low in 1879-82, and then began to rise in 1883. Membership figures took longer to recover, after falling in the period 1878-84 they only rose slightly before stabilising in the years 1886-8. Middleton Foresters recruited only two new members in 1879, none in 1881 and only one in 1883 and membership dropped steadily from 183 in the years 1876-8 to 157 in 1885, a net loss of sixty-nine members in the decade. Funds, which had risen in all but one year since 1845, also declined from £1337 in 1876 to £1168 in 1887.[79] Cranswick Oddfellows' lodge which had no recruits in 1879, 1881-2, and only one in 1883 saw their membership drop from 108 in 1876 to seventy-six in 1885, a net loss of sixty-eight in the decade.[80] Lockington Foresters' funds declined in 1879 and they had no new members in 1882.[81]

Almost all East Riding villages after 1861 were suffering a drop in population and although this must have affected certain friendly societies its impact was not immediate.[82] The effects of a declining rural population were partly counteracted by the higher wages and fuller employment which enabled a greater number of labourers to join. Wages did increase in all regions of Britain in the second half of the century but in some areas proportionally more than others. In the East Riding weekly wages rose from about 12*s* in 1848-9 to around 18*s* 6*d* in 1898. The rise was greatest up to the early 1870s after which wages fluctuated but falls were usually accompanied by a marked drop in prices. By the 1890s the agricultural labourer was generally better off than he had been earlier in the century and more willing, and able, to pay the club subscription.[83]

Of particular importance to the continued survival of affiliated branches was the age of the new members. What were sought were young members who were likely to pay into the funds without drawing any benefit for twenty or more years. Certain societies were particularly successful in recruiting young labourers in the years 1880-1910.

Table 6: Age at joining Two Foresters' Courts 1838-1920

Middleton Foresters - Age at joining 1838-1920

Age	1838-85		1886-1920	
	No.	%	No.	%
15-19	85	21	76	45
20-24	122	31	50	29
25-39	86	22	19	11
30+	105	26	25	15
Total	398		170	

Hutton Cranswick Foresters - Age at joining 1838-1904

Age	1838-65		1866-85		1886-1904	
	No.	%	No.	%	No.	%
15-19	20	10	85	37	101	55
20-24	98	47	103	45	64	35
25-29	44	21	26	12	11	6
30+	45	22	14	6	7	4
Total	207		228		183	

Source: AOF Middleton and Hutton Cranswick proposition books.

This increased recruitment of young agricultural workers in the last decade of the century was not peculiar to the East Riding, as evidence presented to the Royal Commission on the Aged Poor in 1893 showed.[84] Two Norfolk witnesses, George Edwards and Zacharias Walker, leading agricultural trade unionists, stressed that young labourers were joining the affiliated orders in large numbers and that most joined when aged 16-18, many having belonged previously to juvenile branches. Juvenile societies had existed from the 1840s but they did not become common until the last quarter of the century when they were strongly promoted by the affiliated orders. Most of the larger village and town courts and lodges in the East Riding established juvenile branches in the 1870s-80s.[85] Boys joined at from one to four years until sixteen when they could join a parent branch. In the years 1887-99 thirty-five 16 year-olds transferred from the juvenile to senior branches of Cranswick

Foresters. This was a quarter of the total new members.[86]

After 1900 a greater number of individual East Riding friendly societies experienced a decline in membership although overall friendly society membership was still increasing. Twenty-eight of the fifty-nine societies for which there are figures had a drop in membership between 1900 and 1910 with their average membership falling from 145 to 131. The average membership of the thirty-one growing societies rose from 176 in 1900 to 210 in 1910.[87] The larger societies were expanding at the expense of the smaller village clubs. The latter because of their size were not attracting new members and they were more seriously affected by declining population and the competition of the collecting and deposit societies and life assurance companies. Industrial insurance emerged as a rival to friendly societies around 1850 and the system inaugurated in 1854 by the Prudential, which rapidly became the largest of the companies, provided an attractive alternative to the death benefit of the friendly societies.[88] In 1892 Wilkinson, the assistant commissioner reporting on the East Riding to the Royal Commission on Labour, found that at a well attended meeting of labourers at Beeford two-thirds of those present were insured with the Prudential Life Assurance Company.[89]

Typical of the small village clubs going under was the independent Pride of the Valley lodge at Helperthorpe. In June 1908 they held their sixty-ninth anniversary and the vicar commented in the parish magazine:

> For some considerable time this old-established Benefit Society has languished through numerous withdrawals and lack of new members; and we regret to say that the end appears not far off . . . The history of these small village Societies is not a happy one . . . How many of them have had at last to face what has really been always within measurable distance - compulsory dissolution, when the dwindling treasury could no longer meet the growing claims: income from a limited area steadily shrinking, unavoidable expenses, as steadily increasing - much sick pay - chronic old age cases - many death payments - it is really marvellous how this Club has long managed to survive the inevitable and common lot.[90]

The vicar of Helperthorpe did not help the fortunes of the village club by promoting the National Deposit Friendly Society (NDFS) in the same issue of the magazine.[90] The NDFS, which had strong Anglican connections and was a cross between a savings bank and a non-convivial benefit society, advanced rapidly at the end of the century with national membership rising from 16,290 in 1895 to 68,400 in 1901 and 169,100 in 1907.[92] On 7 August 1908 a 'branch' of the NDFS was successfully established for the Helperthorpe area through the vicar's exertions.[93] Not surprisingly the Pride of the Valley lodge, with only sixteen members and £50 funds, was formally dissolved at the Oddfellows' Arms, Helperthorpe on 20 July 1912.[94] It was no coincidence that five days before the dissolution collections had begun to be taken for National Health Insurance.

Friendly societies had long opposed the introduction of state pensions, non-contributory or contributory, but their increasing financial problems eventually won their support for the measure which was passed in 1908 and implemented from 1 January 1909 which gave the bulk of rural working class men and women aged over seventy up to 5*s* a week. Non-contributory old age pensions clearly helped rather than adversely affected friendly societies but the introduction of contributory health insurance three years later, and the termination of the societies near monopoly in this field, can be seen as marking the end of their principal function and the beginning of their demise.[95]

Initially the National Insurance Act, which became law on 16 December 1911, with collections being made from 15 July 1912 and benefits commencing on 15 January 1913 had a beneficial impact on branches of the affiliated orders. Under the Act they became approved societies for the administration of the state health insurance and thereby received a boost to membership and funds. However the benefits were short-lived. An increase in membership in the years 1910-3 was experienced by thirteen of the nineteen East Riding societies for which there is some information but all nineteen had a significant drop in membership by 1920. Combined membership of these societies rose from 4066 in 1910 to 4549 in 1913-5 and then fell by 20 per cent to 3645 in 1920.[96] Keyingham Foresters was a society whose declining fortunes were helped initially by the health insurance scheme. After twenty years of declining membership the society suddenly expanded with twenty-three initiations in 1912, more than in the whole of the previous decade, but the extra benefits obtainable by friendly society membership were not attractive enough to bring in a single new member in the next eight years and membership fell a further 23 per cent to 181 by 1920.[97] Lund Oddfellows which gained over sixty new members in 1912 saw its membership drop 27 per cent from 389 to 283 in the years 1913-20.[98] Continued rural depopulation, state insurance and pensions, competition of insurance companies and finally the loss of many younger members through death and default during the war hastened the decline of many village societies but a surprising number have lasted, albeit precariously, into the 1980s.[99]

4

The Club and the Village Community

Between 1830 and 1912 there were 320 friendly societies established in the East Riding of which 230 were in rural settlements. Although frequently termed 'village clubs' it must not be assumed that they were small-scale parochial organisations with their membership confined to one particular settlement. This was rarely the case and often over half the members of a thriving 'village' club lived in adjoining settlements or further afield. In practice the majority of members of any friendly society, whether local or affiliated, are recruited in the base settlement or immediate vicinity but because of the high degree of mobility of the rural population this membership is gradually dispersed over a wider area and its area of influence and recruitment similarly enlarges. Table 7 shows the catchment area of eight affiliated branches in their first twenty or thirty years.

Most of the branches recruited the great bulk of their new members from within three miles, Lockington Foresters and Hunmanby Shepherds recruited almost 100 per cent, but Keyingham Foresters' court was an exception. During the years 1858-69 there were 290 members who joined the Keyingham court from thirty-seven townships in South Holderness and Hull. Anniversary services and processions were held in the adjoining parishes of Burstwick and Ottringham and by 1879 stewards had been appointed to deal with the distribution of benefits in Keyingham, Burstwick, Burton Pidsea, Thorngumbald and Hull.[1] Clearly Keyingham Foresters was much more than a village society and it cannot be seen as one of the props

Table 7: East Riding Affiliated Branches: Area of recruitment

Residence of new member	Hunmanby Shepherds 1839-69		Cranswick Foresters 1839-59		Lockington Foresters 1840-59		Ferriby Oddfellows 1845-64	
	No.	%	No.	%	No.	%	No.	%
Village	133	80	119	66	79	57	40	49
Within 3 miles	29	17	34	19	56	41	33	41
3 to 5 miles	3	2	17	9	0	0	6	7
5 to 10 miles	2	1	5	3	4	2	0	0
Over 10 miles	0	0	4	2	0	0	2	3

	Middleton Foresters 1839-59		Lund Oddfellows 1839-69		Keyingham Foresters 1858-69		Cranswick Oddfellows 1861	
	No.	%	No.	%	No.	%	No.	%
Village	102	47	124	41	58	20	18	42
Within 3 miles	88	41	163	54	102	35	20	46
3 to 5 miles	7	3	7	2	67	23	5	2
5 to 10 miles	17	8	5	2	61	21	0	0
Over 10 miles	3	1	5	2	2	1	0	0

Source: Lodge and Court Proposition Books

of an insular village community. Friendly societies like so many other features of Victorian village life crossed the artificial boundaries of parishes and they provided important links between communities rather than bolstering a false insularity. Frequently men chose to join a society in a neighbouring settlement rather than their home village. During the years 1839-84 fifty-four Lund residents chose to join Middleton Foresters' court rather than the thriving Oddfellows' lodge in their own village, conversely in the years 1839-69 sixteen men from Middleton and twenty from Lockington, where there was also a Foresters' Court, joined Lund Oddfellows.[2]

As the century progressed the area of recruitment and residence widened. In the twenty years 1840-59 residents of fourteen East Riding villages joined the Foresters' court at Lockington, 57 per cent from Lockington, 41 per cent from ten villages within three miles and only 2 per cent from further afield. However in the twenty years 1880-99 members joined from thirty-seven villages and the percentage from Lockington dropped to 41 per cent. Thirteen per cent lived over five miles away including nine in Hull who joined in the 1890s. In 1912 the 339 members of Lockington Foresters' court lived in ninety-three English settlements and a third lived over ten miles from the base village. Fifty members lived in Hull, and others in Leeds, Bolton, Scunthorpe, Sheffield, Halifax, Middlesbrough and Barrow-in-Furness.[3] A similar proportion of the 163 members of Lund Oddfellows' lodge, spread over fifty-five places, were living over ten miles from the village in 1920. Sixteen were resident in Hull, nine in Leeds and others in London, Bristol, Liverpool, Barnsley, Doncaster and America.[4]

Although numerous in the countryside, affiliated order friendly society branches were by no means present in all villages, nor were they evenly spread throughout the county. Branches were opened in ninety of the East Riding's 326 rural townships during the years 1834-1900 and in only seventy places were the societies in existence long enough to be of assistance to the majority of members. Why were the orders established in some villages and not in others? What criteria were required for the introduction and expansion of the orders in individual villages and areas?

Writers on rural Nonconformity and rural unrest have posed similar questions in order to explain the incidence of Dissent and 'riots' in the nineteenth-century countryside. Alan Everitt found that Dissent flourished in those rural settlements which were:

> almost all marked by an unusual degree of freedom: freedom either in the sense of comprising many small freeholders, self-employed craftsmen and tradesmen, or some similarly independent group of inhabitants; or else in the sense of being situated well away from the nearest parish church and in many cases far from any manor-house. Amongst the former places were the freeholders' parishes, the decayed markets, the industrial villages, and many 'open' villages with a large labour force in areas of intensive farming.[5]

Similarly in answer to their question 'Why did one village riot whereas its neighbour did not?' Hobsbawm and Rudé provided in *Captain Swing* the following 'profile' of the village disposed to riot:

> It would tend to be above average in size, to contain a higher ratio of labourers to employing farmers than the average, and distinctly higher number of local artisans; perhaps also of such members of rural society as were economically, socially and ideologically independent of squire, parson and large farmer: small family cultivators, shopkeepers and the like. Certainly the potentially riotous village also contained groups with a greater than average disposition to religious independence. So far as landownership is concerned, it was more likely to be 'open' or mixed than the rest. Local centres of communication such as markets and fairs were more likely to riot than others . . . We need hardly add that it was more likely to be engaged in tillage and especially grain farming, or in the production of specialized crops with a highly fluctuating demand for labour, and less likely to be engaged in pastoral farming.[6]

It was in just such independent 'open' or mixed villages where the ownership of the housing was not dominated by one or two large landowners that the affiliated orders made their greatest impact in the East Riding. The presence of many agricultural labourers and a high proportion of craftsmen and tradesmen were vital elements for the extent and success of the affiliated orders. The classic 'closed' village was rarely the base for a successful affiliated branch. Of the forty-nine East Riding townships where long lasting branches were established in the years 1834-50 eight (16 per cent) can be broadly described as closed and forty-one (84 per cent) as open. A ring of fourteen townships around Bridlington without affiliated order branches contained thirteen townships that could definitely be classed as closed rather than open. Similarly of a group of thirty-two adjoining townships in the north-west of the county without affiliated branches twenty-six were closed.[7]

Of closed settlements the sub-category of estate villages were the more likely to have affiliated branches as they were to have inns and Methodist chapels. The estate villages of Bishop Burton, Warter, Ganton, and Langton all had branches that lasted into the twentieth century. Sometimes in such settlements the resident landowner provided a 'local society' but not always with great success. Escrick south of York was a large village entirely owned by the Wenlock family. Although they did not allow the building of a Methodist chapel the Wenlocks did rebuild the church and provided a school, allotments and in 1872 a co-operative store. This paternalism had led them also to found, in 1851, the Ouse and Derwent Friendly Society at the adjoining village of Riccall. The society, which was transferred to 'Lord Wenlock's schoolroom' at Escrick in 1856, had 216 members by 1870. Following its initial success the society, which usually had a member of the Wenlock family as one of the trustees, stagnated and no new members were admitted after 1880. Steady decline in membership and funds led to its closure in 1909 when it had only twenty-five members and funds of just under £21.[8]

The paternalism and stagnation of Escrick contrasts with the independence and vitality of the friendly societies in the large open village of Nafferton two miles north-east of Driffield. Here there were lodges of the IOOF MU and the LOAS, founded in 1838 and 1841 respectively, as well as a lodge of the Ancient Order of Shepherdesses established in 1846. All three lodges were still in existence in 1862 when it was remarked in the local newspaper that 'Nafferton can boast of possessing numerous clubs, most of them being in a healthy and prosperous condition'.[9] By this date there was also another Oddfellows lodge was well as an independent Mutual Friendly Society. The township of Nafferton which contained 1260 inhabitants in 1851 covered some 4300 acres of land stretching six miles from the Wolds in the north to the Plain of Holderness in the south. In the mid nineteenth century much of this area was arable and in a 'high state of cultivation'.[10] In 1861 the agricultural workforce, in addition to thirty farmers and a number of family farmworkers on the smallholdings, consisted of 109 agricultural labourers living chiefly in the village and fifty-five farm servants 'living-in' on the larger farms.[11] In 1850 the vicar remarked that the village had been 'long considered as one of the strongholds of Dissent' and it had three chapels, Wesleyan, Primitive and a union of Baptists and Independents.[12] It was estimated in 1868 that there were about 700 dissenters in the parish; 50 per cent of the population.[13] The incumbent in 1850 complained that he had 'no Squire to lend me his help, but the disadvantage of a great number of small independent freeholders'.[14] It was these independent freeholders that gave the village its 'open' character. In the 1868 election twenty-one of the sixty-two resident voters showed an independence uncommon in the area by voting for the Liberal, Haworth; fourteen 'plumping' for him.[15] Among those who plumped for Haworth was Thomas Ward, secretary of the Ancient Order of Shepherdesses, a grocer and draper. Ward had replaced William Laybourn, tailor and draper, as secretary of the Shepherdesses and for many years the secretary of the Shepherds' lodge was a shoemaker and Wesleyan, Israel Jefferson.[16] In 1861 a third of the occupied males in Nafferton were tradesmen or craftsmen, including seventeen shoemakers, sixteen joiners and wheelwrights, fourteen tailors, eleven blacksmiths, eleven bricklayers, eight grocers and drapers, and five saddlers.[17] Accommodation for the numerous friendly societies was initially provided by the four inns and two beerhouses in the village in 1840 but in 1861 the Shepherds built their own hall.[18] Nafferton could not be more typical of an affiliated order village. Other examples are provided in the case studies of Keyingham, Hutton Cranswick and Lund appended to this chapter.

In common with Hobsbawm and Rudé's riotous villages, the East Riding village where an affiliated branch was likely to be established would be more open than closed, was larger than the average, had a higher than average proportion of craftsmen and shopkeepers, had one or more alehouses and one or more Methodist chapels. Not one of the ninety settlements where affiliated branches were opened in 1834-1900 was without an inn in 1840 and only four villages had no Methodist chapel in the mid-nineteenth century. Similarly the majority of these villages were well supplied with craftsmen. In the settlements where the orders were successful in the early period there was an average of ten craftsmen in 1840 comprising three to four shoemakers, two to three tailors, two blacksmiths and two wheelwrights.[19]

Having determined the type of village where an affiliated branch might be established one needs to ask on whose initiative was the order introduced into the settlement? Who decided whether it would be a Foresters' court, an Oddfellows' lodge or a Druids' gorsedd? No reason why any of the groups of East Riding villagers chose to join a particular order has been found but there are indications that the initiative frequently came from existing branches who wished to promote their particular order in the neighbourhood.

'Missionaries', official and unofficial, also travelled the country advocating the cause.[20] There had to be someone in the village who accepted the overtures and gathered together others so that application could be made for a certificate of establishment known as a 'dispensation' or 'surance' from the order headquarters. The names of the founder members of forty AOF courts, one IOOF MU lodge, and one LOAS lodge are available and using the 1841 census enumerators' returns details of the age, occupation and family size of 102 of them have been ascertained.

The evidence from the census returns suggests that the typical founder member was in his mid-thirties, married with three or more children at home.

Innkeepers and their sons understandably figure prominently among the founders of branches of the affiliated orders and in many cases where they do not appear amongst the early members they are also likely to have been the prime mover. Of the forty-four courts opened nationally by the Ancient Order of Foresters in the three months August-October 1839, half had as one of the three or four founders the publican of the inn where the court met.[21] There was some disquiet expressed by the Chief Shepherd of the Loyal Order of Ancient Shepherds at the annual meeting in 1836 for he thought 'That many Lodges were opened more for the gratification of the host than upon those genuine principles which they ought to be'.[22] This was fully acknowledged by Charles Hardwick, a leading propagandist for the affiliated orders, who was of the opinion that many lodges and courts had been opened 'chiefly through the instrumentality of publicans with a view to the improvement of their business'.[23] The great boom in affiliated order expansion in the 1830s and 1840s coincided with a period of greatly increased competition between drinking places consequent upon the passing of the Beer Act in 1830. This Act had broken the monopoly of the licensed victuallers and created the beerhouse. From 1830 any householder paying poor rate could obtain a licence to sell beer on payment of two guineas without the necessity of applying to receive a magistrates licence. The Act, which was partly aimed at reducing the quantity of spirits drunk, led to a proliferation of drinking places and competition for customers. Hosting a friendly society could bring a number of benefits to the publican not least the annual feast and the sales of drink before and after the fortnightly or monthly meeting as well as securing the regular custom of members.

Table 8: Occupations of the Founder Members of 42 East Riding Affiliated Order Branches 1837-43

	No.	%
AGRICULTURE	37	36
Agricultural labourer	24	24
Farm servant	1	
Gardener	2	
Hind	1	
Farmer	7	
Farmer's son	2	
CRAFTS	39	38
Shoemaker	12	12
Wheelwright/joiner	8	
Blacksmith	6	
Tailor	4	
Machine maker (agric.)	1	
Whitesmith	1	
Bricklayer	5	
Plumber/glazier	1	
Stone mason	1	
TRADES	24	24
Innkeeper	10	10
Innkeeper's son	3	
Miller	3	
Butcher	2	
Grocer/draper	2	
Shopkeeper	1	
Fruiterer	1	
Jobber	1	
Coal dealer	1	
CLERICAL/PROFESSIONAL	2	2
Clerk	1	
Schoolmaster	1	
Total	102	100

Sources: AOF Dispensation Book 1, AOF Headquarters, Southampton; HCRO DDX/242 Hunmanby Shepherds; Lund IOOF Minute book, Oddfellows Hall, Lund; Microfilm of 1841 Census Returns, Beverley Library.

The importance of the innkeeper as founder of friendly societies must not be overstated at the expense of the village craftsman. Shoemakers, tailors, blacksmiths, and wheelwrights all figure prominently as founder members and their workshops vied with the inn as the focal point of the village. Information on the expanding affiliated orders was equally likely to enter the village via the shoemaker's shop as by way of the inn. Hobsbawm emphasises that 'the shoemaker was strategically well-placed to pass on city ideas and mobilize action':

> His village shop provided an ideal setting for the purpose, and articulate men who worked alone most of the time might grow loquacious in company, and could do so while they worked. The rural shoemaker was always present, his eyes on the street, and he knew what went on in the community, even when he did not happen to double as parish clerk or in some other municipal or communal capacity. Moreover their quiet workshops in villages and small towns were social centres second only to the inn, open and ready for conversation all day.[24]

Shoemaking was much the largest single artisan occupation in Britain in the mid-nineteenth century. The ubiquity of the shoemaker and his undeniable articulateness and intellectual bent gave him the role of local spokesman and leader in villages in many countries and centuries and this position is one that he clearly held in the East Riding village in the nineteenth century particularly in relation to the more independent organisations. At one time there were twenty-one shoemakers serving as Primitive Methodist local preachers in the Driffield and Bridlington circuit.[25] The shoemaker was similarly prominent in the affairs of the village club.

Table 9 shows that the leadership of the shoemaker was however challenged in many villages by the other craftsmen, particularly the wheelwright, blacksmith and joiner and also that other village intellectual, the schoolmaster.

Table 9: Occupations of Secretaries of Oddfellows' Lodges and Foresters' Courts in the East Riding 1868-96

Shoemaker	11	
Joiner/wheelwright	9	
Schoolmaster	7	
Builder/bricklayer	4	
Blacksmith	3	
Gardener	2	
Tailor	1	
Malster	1	
Lodging house keeper	1	
Parish clerk	1	
Chemist	1	
Farmer	1	
Agricultural labourer	1	Total 42

Sources: IOOF Lodge and AOF Court Directories; Trade Directories; Census Returns

The majority of the lodges and courts of the affiliated orders had procedures for half-yearly elections for all their officers and in the early years it was customary for each position to change hands at this time. In theory no one person or group of people could gain control of the society's affairs but clearly the position of secretary was usually held by a village craftsman. Of the thirty-five men recorded in Table 10 who filled the office of secretary in the adjoining village clubs at Middleton, Lund and Lockington, nineteen were village craftsmen and they served for sixty-one of the 101 'electoral' periods.

As the natural leaders emerged certain members became semi-permanent office holders though continuing to be re-elected each half-year. The posts of secretary and treasurer were the first to become permanent positions and it was these two officers along with the trustees and/or a committee that ran the societies rather than those who filled the positions with the more exalted titles of Chief Ranger, Noble Grand, Arch Druid and Worshipful Master. Among the longer serving secretaries of Middleton Foresters can be cited a wheelwright for thirteen years and a shoemaker for seventeen. William Clark a wheelwright was secretary of Hunmanby Shepherds 1879-88 and Keyingham Foresters' had two shoemaker secretaries in

Table 10: Occupations of 'Elected' Secretaries of Three East Riding Village Clubs

	Middleton AOF 1839-52		Lund IOOF 1839-60		Lockington AOF 1840-90		Total	
	*No.	Times	No.	Times	No.	Times	No.	Times
Blacksmith	2	10	2	3	3	16	7	29
Shoemaker			2	3	2	11	4	12
Miller	1	6			1	6	2	12
Schoolmaster	1	1	1	4	2	5	4	10
Wheelwright			3	8			3	8
Tailor					3	8	3	8
Agric. Lab.			2	2	3	4	5	6
Farmer	2	3	1	1			3	4
Gardener					1	4	1	4
Jobber					1	4	1	4
Saddler	1	1					1	1
Tinner	1	1					1	1
Total	8	22	11	21	16	58	35	101

*No. refers to number of individuals and Times is total number of times people from that occupation were 'elected' to position of secretary.
Sources: Middleton and Lockington AOF and Lund IOOF minute books

the years 1880-1912 and in the same period Hutton Cranswick Oddfellows was served by two shoemakers, William Duke, 1890-1901, and Richard Milner, 1902-12.[26] One of the most obvious choices for secretary was the schoolmaster who would have long been considered the village scribe and accounts keeper. Frequently the schoolmaster was also the parish clerk as was John Robinson the first secretary of Lund Oddfellows. At least ten East Riding village schoolmasters served for a period as the secretary of a village affiliated order branch; some like Robinson and William Woodmansey, secretary of Harpham Druids were 'untrained' but others like George Rayner, secretary of Hutton Cranswick Oddfellows 1877-87, and Thomas Amos, secretary of Holme on Spalding Moor Foresters, had been to a training college and held a certificate.[27]

The village craftsmen dominated the position of club secretary and treasurer and few agricultural labourers were appointed to these positions. The craftsman's centrally placed workshop and his opportunity to be available for friendly society business during the working day gave him great advantages, as club secretary or treasurer, over the more mobile agricultural labourer out on a distant farm from dawn to dusk. Within the friendly society the agricultural labourer could still aspire to the less demanding and more honorary position of the chief officer of the branch or district which generally continued to be chosen half-yearly or annually and in this role he is more fairly represented. In the years 1859-78 ten labourers served as Noble Grand of the Farmer's Refuge Lodge of the Independent Order of Oddfellows at Long Riston, three of them serving three times and two twice. It was usual for a member to fill a number of minor offices in succession before becoming Noble Grand.[28]

A considerable number of agricultural labourers did hold high office in the various branches but it is noticeable that the more lowly the office the greater the likelihood of their appointment.

The open village with a large number of resident agricultural labourers and independent craftsmen was the obvious base for an affiliated order friendly society. The labourers and craftsmen depended on physical ability to work for their livelihood, and illness and old age threatened them and their families with the spectre of the workhouse and so naturally they were attracted to joining a friendly society. In turn the skills and stability of the craftsmen and the numbers of labourers provided both the leadership and membership necessary for a well run and long lasting society. Examples of such societies, which have lasted almost 150 years, are to be found in the three villages examined in the following case studies, Keyingham, Hutton Cranswick and Lund.

Table 11: Occupations of those holding Chief and Vice-office in Four East Riding Affiliated Branches 1839-90

	Lockington Foresters 1840-90		Long Riston Oddfellows 1859-78		Hunmanby Shepherds 1879-88		Lund Oddfellows 1839-80		Total	
Occupation	*No.	Times	No.	Times	No.	Times	No.	Times	No.	Times
CHIEF OFFICE										
Labourer	1	3	10	18	2	2	9	20	22	43
Tailor	1	4	2	6	1	2	3	3	7	15
Blacksmith	2	27	0	0	0	0	4	8	6	35
Shoemaker	1	2	0	0	1	4	3	6	5	12
Wheelwright/ Joiner**	1	1	1	2	0	0	7	11	9	14
Bricklayer	1	2	0	0	0	0	3	5	4	7
Farmer	2	4	0	0	0	0	1	1	3	5
Others	4	12	2	2	5	5	3	6	14	25
VICE-OFFICE										
Labourer	5	25	11	20	2	2	17	24	35	71
Tailor	3	9	2	4	3	3	3	3	11	19
Blacksmith	0	0	1	1	0	0	5	9	6	10
Shoemaker	5	17	0	0	1	1	3	5	9	23
Wheelwright/ Joiner**	1	1	1	1	0	0	8	8	10	10
Bricklayer	0	0	0	0	0	0	2	3	2	3
Farmer	1	3	0	0	0	0	2	2	3	5
Others	2	2	1	1	3	3	3	4	9	10

*No. stands for no. of individuals/Times for no. of times served
** carpenters also included in this category
The offices are Chief and Sub-Chief Ranger (Foresters), Noble and Vice-Grand (Oddfellows) and Worshipful and Deputy Master (Shepherds)
Sources: Minute books of branches

CASE STUDIES

Keyingham

In 1839 the Independent Order of Oddfellows, Manchester Unity and the Ancient Order of Foresters opened branches in the large

Holderness village of Keyingham. Keyingham, a parish of 3210 acres, lies some ten miles east of Hull. Its population of 746 in 1851 made it the second most populous township in South Holderness.[29] In 1832 there were twenty-eight landowners, three of whom, all non-resident, paid 86 per cent of the land tax, 11 per cent of the tax being paid by fourteen owner-occupiers.[30] The estates of the two chief landowners were almost solely confined to the marshland area to the south and housing in the village was largely in the hands of the smaller proprietors which gave the settlement the character of an open village.[31] Half the employed males in 1851 were agricultural workers, and almost a third were craftsmen or tradesmen. There were fifteen shoemakers, seven tailors, six joiners, six blacksmiths and three wheelwrights.[32] In 1840 there was one inn and three beerhouses in the village and chapels belonging to the Wesleyans and Primitive Methodists were built in 1848 and 1846 respectively replacing ones of 1807 and 1823.[33]

The religious census of 1851 shows that Nonconformity was strong at Keyingham with the combined attendances at the Primitive and Wesleyan Methodist chapels exceeding that at the Anglican church. In 1894 the then vicar, J.S. Thomlinson, complained of: 'The prevalence of Dissent which has long existed and which my predecessor, who was Vicar for over 50 years, helped to foster by himself attending the Wesleyan services.'[34]

Court Friendship of the Ancient Order of Foresters was opened at the Ship Inn on 29 June 1839 by nine officers of Court Angel from Hull.[35] At first it developed slowly having only forty-five members in 1845 but in the mid-1850s it rapidly expanded and had 280 members by 1860, 400 by 1870, and a peak of 433 in 1879.[36] It recruited widely in South Holderness and a high proportion (78.5%) of the membership in the period 1861-9 were agricultural workers. The leadership of the court was however usually provided from the 18 per cent who were village craftsmen. In 1868 the secretary was Samuel Pearson, bootmaker and in 1896 it was F. Ford, shoemaker and the treasurer was F. Calvert, blacksmith.[37] The trustees of the court in 1876 were Robert Wreathall, druggist, George Willingham and Richard Andrew, both blacksmiths.[38] The last named who joined the court in 1841 was also the trustee and steward of Burstwick Primitive Methodist Chapel.[39]

There was a close association between the Foresters' and

Methodism, particularly Primitive Methodism. The third anniversary service of the court, and the first where a venue is recorded, was conducted at the Primitive Methodist Chapel at Keyingham in June 1843.[40] At least twenty-five members who joined before 1875 have been identified as Primitive Methodists including seventeen agricultural labourers.[41] The lives of two of the leading trustees of the court in the late nineteenth and early twentieth century, Henry Clark and Richard Westmorland, illustrate well the links with Methodism.

HENRY CLARK (*c.* 1832-1902), shoemaker and grocer, was born at Keyingham. He joined the Foresters in 1855 and held a number of offices before becoming a trustee in 1876. He was a Wesleyan local preacher by 1871 and a leading figure in the Wesleyan chapel. In 1873 he was elected to the newly formed Keyingham school board and, except for the years 1897-9, he served until his death in 1902. He was chairman of the board 1881-2, and 1891-7, and vice-chairman 1888-91 and 1900-2. There were only three contested elections for the board and in 1891 and 1897 he came top of the poll and in 1900 third.[42] In 1891 he received 161 votes while the vicar, Thomlinson, came seventh with forty votes and lost his place on the board to which he had been co-opted in 1881.[43] The second place with 127 votes went to Westmorland. RICHARD WESTMORLAND (*c.* 1847-1936) shoemaker, was born at Marshchapel, Lincolnshire. He was living at Keyingham by 1869 when he joined the Foresters. He held office in the court on a number of occasions and was a trustee of the society 1900-36. An active member of the Primitive Methodist Connexion; he was a local preacher for fifty-nine years, a class leader and chapel steward for forty-eight years, and a Sunday School worker for fifty-two years. In 1884-6 he was chosen as parish constable by the parish vestry but the post lapsed on the appointment of a full-time policeman. He was appointed a member of the Keyingham School Board in an uncontested election in 1888. He served until the dissolution of the board in 1903, being chairman 1897-1900. He was seemingly popular in the community and in the only three contested elections for the board he came second in 1891, fifth in 1897 and fourth in 1900. In 1903 Westmorland along with other local Primitive Methodists refused to pay the Education rate and became a 'passive-resister'. In 1904 however he was one of the County Council appointments as a manager of the school.[44]

The Aeneas lodge of Oddfellows opened at Keyingham in January 1839 and had sixty members by 1845 but it barely exceeded this figure in the next forty years when its membership began to decline. It is last recorded in 1900 when it had a membership of thirty-three and £985 in funds.[45] The lodge originally met at the Blue Bell but in 1876 it purchased the former National School for an Oddfellows' Hall.[46] The membership was drawn from a more exclusive group than that of the Foresters. Over half its membership in 1875 was occupied in light labour, the great majority not exposed to the elements, and it had links with the Anglican church.[47] The leading figure in the lodge was GEORGE KENDALL (1822-1900), National schoolmaster *c.* 1850-76, clerk of the school board, clerk of parish council, assistant overseer of the poor, churchwarden and sidesman for twenty-six years.[48]

Hutton Cranswick

Hutton Cranswick is a township consisting of two distinct settlements the smaller of which, Hutton, lies to the north clustered around the parish church. Cranswick, half a mile to the south, is much more extensive and has at its centre a large green. The township contains 4710 acres and in 1851 its population was 1189.[49] In 1830 the land was held by fifty-nine proprietors with four paying 79 per cent of the land tax.[50] In the mid-nineteenth century the three principal owners, all non-resident, were Lord Hotham, Lord Londesborough and the Reynards of nearby Sunderlandwick Hall.[51] The last attempted, unsuccessfully, to act as squires of Cranswick.[52] There were twenty-three owner-occupiers who chiefly had smallholdings or houses and cottages in Cranswick.[53] In 1851 there were fifteen freeholders and proprietors of houses or land resident in Hutton Cranswick. Some of their property no doubt provided accommodation for the 142 agricultural labourers which constituted 36 per cent of the occupied males in the village, far exceeding the sixty-one farm servants who were less than a third of the agricultural workforce of the parish. Craftsmen were numerous with nineteen shoemakers, fourteen blacksmiths, fourteen tailors, thirteen wheelwrights and eight joiners.[54] In 1840 there was one inn and two beerhouses at Hutton and three inns and two beerhouses at Cranswick.[55] Hutton had a Primitive Methodist chapel and at Cranswick there were Wesleyan, Primitive and Baptist chapels. On Sunday 30 March 1851 the two Primitive chapels recorded the impressive total of 410 attendances - 65 per cent of the total attendances at places of worship in the township, while the Anglican church and Wesleyan chapel had 100 attendances each (16%) and the Baptists only twenty (3%).[56] In 1865 the vicar, Joseph Rigby, in answer to a question from the archbishop on the number of dissenting chapels wrote: 'Alas! There are three. The Independents, The Methodist and The Ranters places - The Masses being steeped in Poverty and Ignorance frequenting these Schismatic Displays as they would theatres.' The average number of the Anglican church congregation was only 'forty or fifty' but the vicar claimed 'they are people of some standing and education and are steady attenders'.[57]

A school board was established in 1872 as school provision in the village was inadequate. The first school board consisted of E.H. Reynard, who was appointed chairman, two farmers, a grocer and John Hobson Wardell, mole killer. At the first meeting Reynard suggested that the curate Revd C.D.Pudsey be appointed secretary but this proposal received no support from the other members. The following year a proposal by Reynard that the girls' school, hitherto provided by his wife, should be taken over by the Board was also rejected by the rest of the members and from that date 'Squire' Reynard took no part in the running of the school. Nonconformists, particularly Primitive Methodists, played an important role in the early management of the school board. At the first election for which voting figures are given, in April 1878, the retiring chairman Robert Dosser, tailor, grocer, and Primitive Methodist local preacher easily topped the poll. In 1887 and 1890 Dosser stood again and was re-elected but on the last occasion only just as he came seventh out of seven. Above him in the poll were three other Primitive Methodists including Singleton Bowes, Chief Ranger of Court Hotham, Ancient Order of Foresters and William Duke, secretary of St Paul's lodge, Independent Order of Oddfellows.[58]

SINGLETON BOWES (1850-1909), blacksmith, was born at Cranswick, the son of a blacksmith and Primitive Methodist lay preacher. He joined Cranswick Foresters in 1872 and was appointed Junior Woodward in 1878 and Chief Ranger in 1880 and he held this latter post for twenty-five years. As noted above he was a leading Primitive Methodist and a member of Cranswick School Board. At the first parish council election in 1894 he came top of the poll. He also sat on the Driffield District Council and was a Poor Law Guardian.[59] WILLIAM DUKE, (*c.* 1843-*c.*1910), shoemaker, was born at Seaton near Hornsea. He was married and living at Lund by 1868 and he joined Lund Oddfellows lodge in May 1875 in which year he was elected a lodge trustee. He was chairman of the trustees in 1876, Vice-Grand 1877 and Noble Grand in 1878. Duke moved to Hutton Cranswick in 1883 and transferred to Cranswick Oddfellows' lodge. In 1888 he was nominated as a trustee of the lodge but was not elected. He was secretary of the lodge 1889-1901. Duke was a leading figure at Cranswick Primitive Methodist chapel and he had been a local preacher since 1868. In 1893 he entertained the President of the Primitive Methodist Conference at his home. As well as being a shoemaker Duke kept four cows which provided milk, that was sold at the door, and butter, which was sold at the village shop. A Liberal he was actively involved in village politics. He failed on his first attempt to get elected to the Cranswick School Board in 1887 when he received seventy-one votes and came tenth out of fourteen candidates for the seven places. Three years later he was elected, coming fifth in the poll with 114 votes. A member of the parish meeting he became the first chairman of Hutton Cranswick Parish Council in 1894 and worked hard to acquire allotments in the village. His sons John and Walter served as treasurer, assistant secretary and trustee of the Oddfellows' lodge in the early twentieth century.[60]

The two affiliated friendly societies along with the Methodist and Baptist chapels dominated the life of Cranswick. Court Hotham, AOF, was opened at the Pack Horse in February 1839 and by 1846 it had a membership of 101. Numbers however dropped to sixty-two in 1852 before rising again in the 1860s. There were 125 members by 1870, 216 in 1880, 259 in 1890 with a peak of 341 in 1910.[61] This last figure was over twice the membership of St Paul's lodge, IOOF MU in that year which numbered 157. The lodge had been opened in 1861, largely it seems at the behest of Watton and Cranswick members of St Peter's lodge, IOOF MU, Lund. The lodge, which is still in existence, had seventy-six members in 1871, ninety-two in 1881, 105 in 1900 and a peak of 180 in 1913.[62] The third affiliated society to appear at Cranswick was not successful. A 'surance' was issued by the Loyal Order of Ancient Shepherds in June 1842 for the opening of the Shepherd's Refuge lodge of the order at the Cross Keys Inn but no further mention of it has been found.[63] Although, as usual, the Oddfellows seem to have attracted a more professional and upper artisan element than the Foresters there was little difference in the occupational and social structure of their overall membership. Seventy-two per cent of the 600 men who joined the AOF court in 1838-99 were agricultural workers and 22 per cent were craftsmen and tradesmen, and 75 per cent of the 165 who joined the IOOF lodge in 1861-80 were agricultural workers and 18 per cent craftsmen and tradesmen.[64] There were four schoolmasters who joined the Oddfellows in this period including George Rayner, (1844-1927), the master of the board school, who was secretary to the lodge 1877-87 and then trustee from 1888.[65] In contrast secretaries of the Foresters' court included two labourers, Robert Sissons 1847-62, and Robert Moody 1888-9, and a hairdresser, James Robson 1891-8.[66] Although founded in public houses both societies eventually acquired their own halls overlooking Cranswick Green. In 1863 the Oddfellows' bought the former Wesleyan chapel and converted it to their hall and in 1901 the Foresters' built their large hall further along the street.[67] These halls were the centres of the celebrations of the annual feasts which disrupted village life and closed the board school for a week each June.[68] On occasions the societies paraded together but more often they celebrated their anniversaries independently.[69]

Lund

Lund lies on the edge of the Wolds seven miles north-west of Beverley. The parish which covers an area of 3078 acres had a population of 503 in 1851.[70] The twenty-four proprietors of land in 1830 included ten owner occupiers who paid 11.5 per cent of the land tax but the greater part of the parish was in the hands of four non-resident landowners, Charles Grimston, John Broadley, William Binnington and the Duke of Devonshire who between them paid 70 per cent of the land tax.[71] By 1850 the Duke of Devonshire's land was owned by Lord Londesborough and in 1872 Lord Hotham purchased the manor and estate formerly the property of the Broadleys.[72] In 1851 there were ninety-nine agricultural workers, fifty-five of them labourers and forty-four farm servants and they constituted 58 per cent of the occupied males in the parish, craftsmen and tradesmen provided a further 22 per cent. The craftsmen included seven tailors, six shoemakers, six blacksmiths and six wheelwrights. The two publicans recorded kept the Duke of Wellington and the Plough.[73]

Lund was strongly Nonconformist in the mid-late nineteenth century. Indeed in 1894 the vicar complained of the 'Utter indifference of the people. Not a real Churchman among the whole population. This is the result of past years'.[74] Although the lack of support for the Anglican church is not then evident the strength of Methodism is borne out by the religious census returns of 1851. The average total attendances at the parish church are given as 160, and the total attendances on Sunday 30 March at the Wesleyan and Primitive Methodist chapels were 90 and 80 respectively.[75] The former chapel was built in 1835 and the latter in 1839.[76] Primitive Methodism was particularly successful in Lund with membership rising from eight in 1839, to forty-one in 1853 and fifty-six in 1869.[77] In 1887 it was said that a third of the adult population were attenders at the Primitive chapel and at one time there were eight local preachers resident in the village.[78]

St Peter's lodge, IOOF, MU, which was opened in August 1839 at the Wellington Inn, had as its first secretary John Robinson (1789-1871) National schoolmaster and parish clerk.[79] There were seventy-one members by 1845, 146 in 1865 and 1875, 213 in 1895 and a peak of 392 in 1912.[80] Agricultural workers provided 76 per cent of the new members in the years 1868-79 and 75 per cent of the total membership of 287 in 1903-4.[81] The lodge met at the Wellington Inn until 1924 when the former Primitive Methodist chapel, which had become a temperance hall, was purchased and became the Oddfellows' Hall.[82] Although the lodge had many Primitive Methodists among its members and officers it showed no clear sign of partisanship. The anniversary services were always held at the parish church, and for many years the feast was presided over by the vicar, Revd A. Grimston, with a Wesleyan farmer Robert Prescott in the vice-chair and the Primitive Methodist secretary organising the proceedings.[83]

The secretary was WILLIAM PETCH (*c*. 1826-1919) of Lund and Middleton-on-the-Wolds, wheelwright and builder. Born at

Goodmanham, the son of a shopkeeper/smallholder, he was apprenticed to a wheelwright at Lund, Richard Vary, whose daughter he married in 1847. Vary (*c.* 1806-88), an Anglican, was treasurer of the Oddfellows' lodge 1853-80 and served as Noble Grand on more than one occasion and as Deputy Grand Master to Beverley District. William Petch joined Lund Oddfellows' lodge in July 1853 and was immediately appointed secretary. He was re-elected to this position five times before being made permanent secretary in 1860 a post he retained until 1893. He filled the office of Noble Grand in 1854 and 1858, was a lodge trustee from February 1860 and had been Provincial Deputy Grand Master by August 1858. He exercised a considerable influence over the society for some fifty years and is commemorated by a coloured portrait photograph which still hangs in the Oddfellows' Hall at Lund.[84]

Petch moved to Middleton on the Wolds in 1857 and there he became the leading figure in the Primitive Methodist chapel. He was chapel steward, trustee, class leader and a local preacher from *c.* 1859. Woodcock pays the following tribute to him in *Piety Amongst the Peasantry*:

> Mr Wm Petch, who, as builder and architect, has done much to improve our Wolds chapels, is a man of good abilities and sterling character; . . . even, steady, consistent, thorough; and who has represented the circuit at District Meetings and Conference, has been our leading official here [Middleton] for many years. He and his wife entertain one of the preachers, and for years their daughter played the harmonium at our chapel.[85]

In 1894 Petch was elected a member of the first parish council at Middleton.[86]

5

Membership and Benefits

The limited attention that has been paid to friendly societies can partly be attributed to a widely held view that they contributed only marginally to the welfare and economy of the bulk of the working-class in nineteenth-century Britain. This view derives from the statements made by many writers who confine membership of friendly societies to 'the aristocracy of the wage earning classes', 'the upper working and lower middle class' or 'small tradesmen and artisans'.[1] Bentley Gilbert in a much quoted passage expressed the opinion that 'Friendly society membership was traditionally the badge of the artisan. The grey, faceless, lower one-third of the British working population lay altogether outside their province.'[2] The sources of such statements can be traced back either to Gosden's chapter on the 'Social composition of the membership and leadership' in *The Friendly Societies in England* or directly to the evidence given to various Royal Commissions, in particular that relating to Friendly Societies in the early 1870s.[3] In the reports of this Commission friendly society members were stated to be 'rather a respectable class - what are called respectable artizans', 'mechanics and tradesmen', 'very largely of the mercantile class, clerks, and warehousemen, and the skilled artizan class', 'of the ordinary artizan class', 'for the most part handi-craftsmen'.[4] The Commission also heard evidence from an official of the IOOF MU who was of the opinion that no Oddfellow earned less than 20*s* a week and that the membership was 'Generally the more respectable class of tradesmen and clerks; it embraces also some in a lower class, but they oftentimes retire from it by non-payment'.[5] This conviction of the predominance of artisan membership has been strengthened by the work that has been done by Gray, Kirk and Crossick on urban societies. R.Q. Gray's analysis of the membership of an Edinburgh lodge of the Scottish Order of Oddfellows in the 1850s-70s reveals 71 per cent of members in the skilled and only 1.5 per cent in semi- or unskilled categories.[6] The membership of an Oddfellows' lodge in Stockport in the 1850s-70s analysed by Kirk showed a 'strong presence of craft, skilled and lower-middle class occupations'.[7] Crossick in his study of Kentish London was able to analyse the occupations of members of twenty-eight Foresters' courts in Woolwich in the period 1845-76. Here 53 per cent of new members were skilled workers and 30 per cent unskilled with the proportion of the latter rising during the period.[8]

In the view of contemporaries the rural unskilled were equally unlikely to join the affiliated orders. Sir George Young in his report on the southern and eastern counties to the Friendly Societies commission stated that 'with few exceptions the lodges of a society like the Manchester Unity were practically closed against agricultural labourers and other unskilled labourers by the high rate of contributions demanded.'[9] Later Commissions produce similar statements. In 1893 a fellow of the Institute of Actuaries, in giving evidence to the Royal Commission on the Aged Poor, stated that friendly societies providing sick pay included:

> not more than one third or one fourth of the workers; they certainly do not include that large mass of pure labour for whom it is most desirable that these schemes should be propounded; they do not take in the dockers and . . . they take in only a very limited proportion of the agricultural labourer, therefore nothing . . . that the friendly societies could do, even if their finances permitted it, would touch the mass of the population of this country.[10]

Included in this mass of population were the agricultural labourers whose wages were rarely above subsistence level and therefore did not have, in the opinion of Peter Mathias, the surplus funds necessary for the support of self-help movements. 'The agricultural labourers had the poorest record of membership of friendly societies, and the highest record of receipts from poor relief funds'.[11]

Such a view can be entirely refuted by an examination of the surviving membership lists and proposition books for individual East Riding societies. These show conclusively that agricultural workers, both labourers and hired farm servants, formed the majority of the membership of affiliated branches in the rural East Riding from their establishment. Full details exist of the occupations of all new recruits to three Ancient Order of Foresters' Courts in the mid-Wolds area of the East Riding for the sixty or so years of their existence in the nineteenth century. Agricultural worker membership of these societies at Middleton, Hutton Cranswick and Lockington ranges from 71 to 76.5 per cent with a marked increase as the century progresses.

Table 12: Occupations of New Members of Three East Riding AOF Courts 1838-99

	Hutton Cranswick 1838-99	%	Middleton 1839-99	%	Lockington 1840-99	%
Agricultural Workers	431	72	322	71	450	76.5
Craftsmen	116	19.5	76	17	85	14.5
Tradesmen	15	2.5	21	4.5	25	4.0
Farmers	20	3.5	15	3.5	9	1.5
Professionals	4	0.5	11	2.0	0	0
Others	14	2.0	8	1.5	18	3.0
Total	600		453		587	

Sources: AOF court proposition books

The above figures can be broken down into three periods which clearly show the increasing proportion of agricultural workers joining the societies.

Table 13: Occupations of New Members at Three Periods.

	Hutton Cranswick	%	Middleton	%	Lockington	%
Early period 1838-59						
Agricultural Workers	102	56.5	142	66	94	69
Craftsmen	49	27	40	19	24	18
Tradesmen	7	4	15	7	11	8
Farmers	19	10.5	9	4	6	4
Professionals	2	1	6	3	0	0
Others	2	1	2	1	1	1
	181		214		136	
Middle period 1860-79						
Agricultural Workers	128	73	101	72	139	77
Craftsmen	40	23	25	18	32	18
Tradesmen	4	2.5	3	3	6	3
Farmers	0	0	3	2	0	0
Professionals	2	1	5	4	0	0
Others	1	0.5	3	2	4	2
	175		140		181	
Later period 1880-99						
Agricultural Workers	201	82.5	79	80	217	80
Craftsmen	27	13.5	11	11	29	11
Tradesmen	4	1.5	3	3	8	3
Farmers	1	0.5	3	3	3	1
Professionals	0	0	0	0	0	0
Others	11	4.5	3	3	13	5
	244		99		270	

Sources: AOF court proposition books

This upward trend in recruitment of agricultural workers continues in the early twentieth century. In the period 1900-19 Middleton Foresters had seventy-three agricultural workers join (90% of new members) and only six craftsmen (7.5%) and two tradesmen (2.5%).[12]

The above statistics are for Foresters' courts and both contemporary and more recent writers have expressed the view that Foresters were more likely to have labourer membership than the Oddfellows. Figures for a variety of lodges and courts in the middle period show however a similar pattern of membership in each.

Table 14: New Members of Affiliated Orders

	Cranswick IOOF MU 1861-80		Lund IOOF MU 1868-79		Hunmanby LOAS 1860-8		Keyingham AOF 1861-9	
		%		%		%		%
Agricultural Workers	124	74	34	75.5	56	73	371	77
Craftsmen	25	15	9	20	17	22	85	18
Tradesmen	5	3	2	4.5	1	1	23	5
Professionals	0	0	0	0	0	0	0	0
Others	10	6	0	0	1	1	2	0

Sources: Branch proposition and minute books

There is a surprising similarity in the figures and this is particularly marked in Hutton Cranswick where there are the parallel figures for the Foresters and Oddfellows which had 128 (73%) and 124 (74%) new agricultural worker members respectively in the middle period.

One of the reasons suggested by Gosden for limited agricultural worker membership was the survival of hirings and living-in in the north, his evidence coming from Northumberland.[13] G. Culley, an Assistant Commissioner for the Royal Commission on Friendly Societies in 1872, and Wilson Fox, an Assistant Commissioner for the Royal Commission on Labour in 1894, both reporting on Northumberland, stated that there were few friendly societies in the rural areas 'probably on account of the farm servants being hired by the year, and their wages being thus secure during sickness'.[14] Farm servants might not seem the most likely candidate for friendly society membership for they were considered to be protected, during service, from financial worries brought on by illness, bad weather, agricultural depression, and a large family. In the East Riding however the hired farm servants were among the most active in joining the affiliated orders.

Table 15: Agricultural Labourer/Farm Servant Membership of Three AOF Courts

	Agricultural Labourers	%	Farm Servants	%	Others	%	Total
Keyingham AOF 1861-69	163	34	202	43	107	22	472
Hutton Cranswick AOF 1869-89	80	31	116	45	60	24	256
Lockington AOF 1880-99	105	39	95	35	70	26	270

Sources: Court proposition books

In the five years 1878-82 sixty-two men joined Hutton Cranswick Foresters; of these forty-nine (79%) were farm servants with an average age of twenty. All but two were single. Most of the large numbers of those aged twenty and under who are classed as labourers in the records of other courts and lodges must also have been hired farm servants. Thirty-seven per cent of the 270 labourers who joined Middleton Foresters 1838-90 were twenty or under and half of these were eighteen and under.[15]

Much of the evidence presented for low agricultural labourer membership comes from the south and east of England. The East Riding agricultural labourer was better paid and more regularly employed than his southern counterpart and this may be a reason why he would be more likely to join a branch of an affiliated order. E.H. Hunt has demonstrated that the regional wage variations were not offset by any marked variation in the cost of living in various parts of the country and that in high wage areas such as the East Riding the standard of living was indeed higher than in the rural southern counties.[16] In 1913 an Oxfordshire labourer earning 14*s* 11*d* a week would have had to pay 3*s* $2^1/_2$d for a pound of butter, a pound of margarine, a pound of sugar, four ounces of tea and seven pound of flour while these items would have cost the same to an East Riding labourer earning 19*s* 3*d*.[17] Thus the 3*d* or 4*d* a week club subscription would have been quite manageable for the East Riding labourer. Evidence however suggests that by the late nineteenth century the high labourer membership in the East Riding was not unusual throughout rural England. The national secretary of the Foresters in giving evidence to the Royal Commission on the Aged Poor in 1895 claimed high agricultural labourer membership in the south of England and a Norfolk agricultural trade union official told the same Commission that his Oddfellows lodge had 420 members of which 360 were agricultural labourers.[18] Investigators for the 1909 Royal Commission on the Poor Law found that registered friendly society membership was highest in rural areas where wages were lowest and the permanent secretary of the AOF told the same commission that some of their orders best branches were in areas with the lowest wages and that they were weakest in the larger towns where wages were high. This was said to be because the lower paid had to think more carefully about how to provide for themselves in the event of sickness. Better paid workers had more alternatives available.[19]

Having established that, in the rural East Riding at least, a large proportion of labourers did belong to a friendly society it must now be considered to what extent their membership was of financial assistance to them and their families.

The financial benefits received by members of affiliated order friendly societies in return for their contributions and special levies were of four main types: regular relief when unable to work through sickness or accident; medical aid; a travelling allowance when seeking work, and a lump sum on the death of the member and member's wife. The contributions and benefits of affiliated branches were surprisingly uniform. Up to the mid-1850s the weekly subscriptions for all members were 4*d*-5*d* per week and in addition the branches had occasional levies for funeral funds and frequently separate contributions for medical aid. An examination of the rule books of twelve East Riding lodges and courts belonging to seven different orders for the years 1851-70 shows that they had a standard sickness benefit of 10*s* per week for the first six months reducing to 5*s*-7*s* 6*d* for the following six months then 3*s* 6*d*-5*s* for the next six months, a year or indefinitely. Four of the branches used their discretion on the rate after eighteen to twenty-four months. The funeral benefit ranged from £10 to £12.[20]

The individual sums paid on sickness and death hardly changed from the late 1830s to the First World War but with increased actuarial experience the chief orders introduced graduated scales of initiation fees and contributions relating to age, or age on joining, from the 1850s.[21] The following tables were in force for a Beverley Foresters' court and Long Riston Oddfellows' lodge in 1859-60; in the case of the Oddfellows' lodge a member was free to receive sickness benefits at the end of six calendar months after the whole of the initiation fee had been paid and funeral money after twelve calendar months. But with the Foresters' court the situation was reversed and it was the funeral money that was obtainable after six months and the sickness benefit after twelve months.

Table 16: Tables of Contributions and Benefits IOOF MU and AOF Branches 1859-60

IOOF MU Farmers' Refuge Lodge, Long Riston 1860

Age at admission	Initiation Fee			Weekly Contribution	Additional Contribution		
	£	*s*	*d*		£	*s*	*d*
18-21	0	5	0	4*d*	0	0	0
22-23	0	5	0	4*d*	0	0	0
24-26	0	7	6	4*d*	0	2	0
27-29	0	10	0	4*d*	0	3	4
30	1	0	0	4*d*	0	4	3
31	1	2	6	4*d*	0	4	3
32	1	5	0	4*d*	0	4	5
33	1	7	6	4*d*	0	5	8
34	1	10	0	4*d*	0	6	7
35-38	1	12	6	4*d*	0	7	6

A contribution of 2*d* (monthly) required from each member to defray necessary expenses of management. Benefits: Sickness - First 26 weeks 10*s* per week, second 26 weeks 7*s* 6*d* per week and remainder of illness 3*s* 6*d* per week; at the death of a member £12, member's wife £10, second wife £3.[22]

AOF Court Beverley, Beverley 1859

Age at admission	Initiation Fee £	s	d	Weekly Contribution	Additional Contribution £	s	d
18-21	0	5	0	4*d*	0	0	0
22-24	0	5	0	4*d*	0	0	6
25-29	0	7	6	4*d*	0	1	0
30	0	10	0	4*d*	0	2	6
31	0	10	0	4*d*	0	3	0
32	0	10	0	4*d*	0	3	6
33	0	10	0	4*d*	0	4	0
34	0	10	0	4*d*	0	4	9
35	0	12	6	4*d*	0	5	6
36	0	12	6	4*d*	0	6	3
37	0	12	6	4*d*	0	7	0
38	0	12	6	4*d*	0	8	0
39	0	12	6	4*d*	0	9	0

Benefits: Sickness - First 26 weeks 10*s* per week, second 26 weeks 6*s* per week and third 26 weeks 3*s* per week; at the death of a member £12, member's wife £10, second wife £6.[23]

Potentially the financial benefits to be received in return for the modest contributions to affiliated branches were considerable. For example a married agricultural labourer who joined Long Riston Oddfellows at the age of twenty-two on 1 January 1859 would probably pay into the lodge funds about £2 8*s* during his first two years membership. If however he was, through illness, incapable of work from 1 January 1860, and on 1 March his wife died and he himself died after a year long illness then he would have received, including the funeral gift to his nearest relative, at least £44 2*s* plus free medical attention in the two years. Fortunately for the branches such an occurrence would be very unusual. However entries in the early contribution and cash books of St. Peter's lodge, IOOF MU, Lund show that some members did receive similar amounts of relief. The great range of contributions and benefits is shown by the twenty-one individual cases tabulated below.

Table 17: Lund Oddfellows: Individual Members' Contributions and Benefit Payments 1839-58

Name	Occupation	Period of Membership	Contributions	Benefits
1. Ben. Cobb	Publican	9/1839-12/1853	£14 - 5*s*	£53 -13*s*8*d*
2. Dan. Dickinson	-	11/1839-8/1843	£3 - 0*s*4*d*	nil
3. Wilson Ward	Ag. lab.	2/1840-8/1858	£18 - 16*s*	£1 -18*s*-4*d*
4. Wm Johnson	Ag. lab.	1/1840-4/1845	£4 - 17*s*-4*d*	nil
5. David Keith	Ag. lab.	12/1839-2/1841	£1 - 2*s*-8*d*	nil
6. Rbt Holdenby	Ag. lab.	11/1839-8/1858	£19 - 3*s*	£12 -10*s*
7. John Robinson	Schoolmaster	9/1839-8/1858	£18 - 18*s*-9*d*	£1 - 3*s*-4*d*
8. Joseph Wade	-	7/1840-9/1854	£14 - 7*s*-4*d*	0 -10*s*
9. Rbt Smith	Ag. lab.	10/1840-2/1841	0 - 5*s*-4*d*	nil
10. Edward Bowser	Ag. lab.	2/1841-8/1858	£17 - 19*s*4*d*	£9 - 0*s*-0*d*
11. Francis Taylor	Ag. lab.	3/1841-2/1852	£10 -12*s*-8*d*	£2 -10*s*
12. Wm Woodall	Ag. lab.	3/1841-8/1858	£18 - 3*s*	nil
13. John Ullyott	Shoemaker	5/1841-8/1858	£17 - 15*s*-2*d*	£8 -10*s*
14. Wm Farmery	Farm servt	4/1841-8/1843	£1 - 5*s*	nil
15. Thomas Cross	Ag. lab.	4/1841-8/1848	£6 - 6*s*-8*d*	£1 -18*s*-4*d*
16. Wm Sleights	Ag. lab.	4/1841-2/1852	£10 - 9*s*-4*d*	£13 - 6*s*-8*d*
17. Geo. Blakeston	Ag. lab.	4/1841-1/1849	£7 - 1*s*-6*d*	£3 -1*s*-6*d*
18. John Ward	Ag. lab.	4/1841-8/1849 *	£7 - 14*s*-6*d*	£13 -0*s*-0*d*
19. Stabler Woodall	Ag. lab.	4/1841-12/1850	£9 - 0*s*-4*d*	£53 -15*s*
20. Thos Arnott	Bricklayer	5/1841-8/1858	£18 - 8*s*-3*d*	£2 - 8*s*-4*d*
21. Richard Vary	Wheelwright	5/1841-8/1858	£18 - 1*s*	£1 -15*s*
Total			£237 - 12*s*-6*d*	£17 -0s2*d*

* died

Sources: IOOF MU Lund, Contribution books 1839-56, 1856-69; Cash book 1839-58.

Of the twenty-one, eight were still members in August 1858, one had died, one had drawn clearance and the other eleven had either been expelled for being in arrears or their membership had lapsed. These eleven included three who received more in benefits than they paid in contributions during their membership. Two, Benjamin Cobb and Stabler Woodall, did exceptionally well and their membership was certainly beneficial to them. Cobb, the publican of the Wellington Inn, was a founder of the lodge and it met at his house. He was already in his early fifties when the lodge opened and it was in

September 1845 that he first received sickness benefit. In 1845 he received £4 from the lodge in eight consecutive weekly payments of 10*s* and then again in 1850 £4 10*s* in consecutive payments. A long term illness commenced at the end of December 1850 and for six months Cobb was granted 10*s* a week, then a further six months at 7*s* a week, and finally over 80 weeks at 3*s* 6*d* per week. During this latter period his wife died and he received £10 funeral benefit for her and by mid-July 1853 he had received a total of £53 13*s* 6*d* from the lodge and contributed less than £14. Cobb, notwithstanding his position as founder and initial host of the lodge, was seemingly not popular and the minute books have frequent references to his case. In March 1851 he had to forfeit one week's sick gift as well as pay a fine of 5s on a charge of being tipsy when in receipt of relief. Five months later it was proposed, though not carried, that Cobb be suspended from all benefits of lodge for breaking some unnamed rule. The same proposal was made in April 1853 and finally on 18 July of that year it was 'unanimously agreed . . . that Brother Benjamin Cobb be struck off from his sick gift'. Cobb took his case to the annual district meeting in December 1853 which decided in his favour, but the lodge appealed to the Grand Master and Board of Directors of the Order. On 9 May 1854 the village wheelwright and lodge treasurer, Past Provincial District Grand Master Richard Vary, appeared before the appeal committee in Manchester but the outcome of the case is not recorded. However by this date Cobb's membership of the order had lapsed through non-payment of his contributions.

Stabler Woodall was seemingly a far more deserving beneficiary although he only paid £9 in contributions and received £53 15*s* in sickness benefit in his nine year membership of the lodge. Woodall, an agricultural labourer from Holme on the Wolds, was only twenty-two when he started receiving sick pay in 1844 which continued until May 1850. His sickness was probably a result of an accident for in 1845 he was in Hull Infirmary. In June 1846 he went, with £5 from the lodge, some thirty miles to Cawood, near Selby, seeking the attention of a medical specialist. This visit was short lived but in March 1848 he was at Pocklington under the care of Dr Thomas Wilson 'for his arm'. In March 1850 Woodall proposed to withdraw himself from the lodge in return for his funeral gift but this was not accepted and the following month the Oddfellows passed the following resolution:

> that Bro. S. Woodall providing he can find employment to watch the cattle in the lanes of Lund still be required to do so; and that his pay shall cease when so employed which he is at present in receipt of weekly - and that after Michaelmas if again out of any employment he shall again be in receipt of his sick gift.

Woodall received his last sickness benefit on 4 May 1850 and was noted to have begun 'tenting' two days later. He made his last contribution to the lodge funds in December 1850 and was excluded for being in arrears the following year.

The third principal beneficiary of the lodge, William Sleights, agricultural labourer, was a member for eleven years during which time he contributed £10 9*s* 4*d* and received £13 6*s* 8*d*. He received sick pay for only 40 days and the bulk of the benefit was the £10 he received when his wife died of cholera at Hedon in August 1849.[24] Similarly it was the benefit for his wife's funeral that made up the bulk of Robert Holdenby's £12 10*s* that he received from the lodge during the years 1839-58. The other major recipient John Ward had only two weeks sick pay in 1842 during the eight years he contributed before dropping down dead in the harvest field in September 1849 when his family received £12 funeral gift.

In the case of eight whose membership lapsed through non-payment, their contributions exceeded the benefits they received by £27 1*s* 6*d*. Francis Taylor, an agricultural labourer of Lund and Bracken, was a member for over eleven years and he contributed regularly until 15 February 1852 from which date he made no more contributions. He had paid in £10 12*s* 6*d* and received forty days sick pay of £2 10*s*. William Johnson received nothing for the £4 17*s* 4*d* he paid in before emigrating to America in 1845. Another agricultural labourer, Thomas Cross, also went to America in 1848, having paid in £6 6*s* 8*d* and received £1 18*s* 4*d* and the lodge secretary John Robinson noted that he was: 'A Ranter Parson and left me in debt for money paid to lodge *Bad Chap* Trumpt up a packet of lies'. However it was from such defaulters as Thomas Cross that the lodge gained important income that helped pay for the increased call upon the funds by those who remained members for the rest of their lives.

In the East Riding in the mid-late nineteenth century the

sickness benefit paid by the affiliated orders constituted a high proportion of the average weekly wage of the agricultural labourer. The East Riding was a so-called 'high' wage area but even with wages at 12*s* to 15*s* a week, the sickness benefit of 10*s* for the first six months illness would account for at least 75 per cent of a labourer's wage.[25] In the short term such help compared well with what was likely from outdoor poor relief, if obtainable. The standard outdoor allowance throughout the Victorian period was around 2*s* 6*d* to 3*s* per week though certain Guardians paid more. In 1837 Beverley Guardians set the scale of out-relief for every male pauper, eating with his family, at 4*s* per week, plus 2*s* for his wife and 1*s* 6*d* for each child.[26]

With rises in wages the value of the basic sickness benefit declined but the rise in wages was not great. In 1892 in the Driffield Poor Law Union area the usual labourer's wages were '15*s* for ordinary weekly men, or 16*s* if doing Sunday work'.[27] By 1912 wages were a little higher but the man's weekly wage in the four East Riding families included in Rowntree's *How the Labourer Lives* only ranged from 15*s* to 18*s*.[28]

Throughout the period 1830-1912 the unchanging basic sickness benefit gave at least half-pay for six months. Those earning more in agriculture or other occupations had two alternatives in order to improve their benefits: they could either join more than one affiliated order or friendly society; or, after 1866, in the case of the IOOF MU, they could increase their contributions in order to get increased benefit.[29] If the member was sick for six months or less the friendly society benefit was adequate. For the long term invalid and the infirm the benefits available after one year, usually from two shillings and sixpence to four shillings a week, were far from adequate and did require supplementing by parish relief which was facilitated in 1894 with the passing of the first Outdoor Relief (Friendly Societies) Act which left it to the discretion of Boards of Guardians as to whether or not friendly society benefits should be taken into account when awarding outdoor relief. This rather unsatisfactory measure was superseded by the 1904 Outdoor Relief (Friendly Societies) Act, promoted by the National Conference of Friendly Societies which allowed an individual to receive up to 5*s* per week from a friendly society and still be eligible for full parish relief. Parish relief was rarely more than the friendly society benefit but it did take into account other members of the family and allowed more freedom of movement and employment.[30]

The strict control of the actions of members who were 'on the box' is one aspect of the management that is well remembered and often criticised. The payment of relief was supervised within the local area by a specially appointed visiting officer or sick steward. The steward, or any other member, was supposed to report to the court or lodge if the person on sick benefit broke any of the branch rules relating to working or leisure pursuits. All the orders had similar rules to the following:

> That no member whilst he is receiving sick pay from this lodge shall be allowed to do any kind of work, or take any violent exercise to aggravate his disease; he shall not be allowed to attend any feast, fair, or races, or be out after 6 o'clock in the evening, in the winter season, or before 9 o'clock in the morning, (that is from September 21st to March 21st), nor later than 9 o'clock in the summer, (that is from March 21st to September 21st), nor before 6 o'clock in the morning, any members violating this rule shall be fined to any amount not exceeding £1, or not less than 2*s* 6*d*, as a majority of the lodge may think proper; and further, shall he be known to be intoxicated whilst he is receiving the sick benefits of this lodge, he shall be fined or expelled as a majority of the lodge may think fit.[31]

Much ill feeling was engendered by the way that men on sick pay were closely watched but it was seen to be in the interests of every member to keep the expenditure on benefits down to the minimum. Many members turned informer on their fellow villagers, even on members of their own family.[32]

Branch minute books abound in cases of people charged with offences in relation to their receipt of sick pay. In 1846 Lund Oddfellows ordered that James Teale, blacksmith, should forfeit the 15*s* sick pay he claimed because it was reported that he had been seen driving a cow.[33] W.H. Beilby of North Ferriby Oddfellows was fined 15*s* in 1868 'for disgraceful conduct in being at a public house until

11 o'clock p.m.' whilst receiving sick relief.[34] In the same year John Whitting, of Skirlaugh, was suspended for three months from the benefits of Long Riston Oddfellows Lodge for absenting himself from home and for chopping sticks, while on sick pay.[35] The prohibition of any type of work when on 'club pay' was particularly restrictive and harsh on the elderly or anyone incapacitated from having a full time job who being in long term receipt of benefit only received two or three shillings. For such men the meagre parish relief was preferable because there was always the possibility of some casual employment. Few clubs, particularly the affiliated branches, made any special provision for those who were not sick but were too old to work. Some however were considered as if they were sick and given long term relief. In the 1880-90s Lockington Foresters granted a pension of three shillings a week to its oldest members and was not averse to them earning a little if they could and receiving parish relief. However if the pensioner was also obtaining parish relief he had to use the parish doctor or pay for one out of his own pocket and could not make use of the court doctor.[36]

Affiliated branches saw medical treatment as an important way of reducing the amount of sick and funeral benefit and soon after their establishment it was usual for them to make contracts with local doctors for the medical care of their members. For this service members usually paid a fixed sum per year additional to their weekly contributions. The minute books of Lund Oddfellows provide details of contracts taken out with the doctors. In 1841 Dr John Wood of Middleton, a prominent Primitive Methodist, undertook to find medicines and treat every sick or lame member for the sum of two shillings and sixpence per head per annum to be paid by every member at the end of each year. If the doctor had to travel over three miles from the lodge he was to have one shilling per mile from the lodge funds. The following year a member charged Dr Wood with neglect and in 1843 Dr William Bulmer of Lund was elected surgeon by a great majority. His contract was for members within five miles of lodge and he was to provide, in addition to medicines, six leeches for each member if needed. All medicine bottles were to be returned or $1^1/_2$d to be paid for each bottle retained unless broken by accident. The medical treatment did not cover any venereal disease or 'hurt by fighting or drunkenness'.[37]

The amount paid per member to the doctor varied from

branch to branch but 2*s* 6*d* to 3*s* was the normal sum although in 1875 Long Riston Oddfellows agreed to pay Dr Calvert of Brandesburton 5*s* per member.[38] Being a club doctor was not necessarily lucrative but it could form the mainstay of a practice. As the clubs grew in size and medical men became more numerous the competition for club contracts in the towns became quite intense with doctors undercutting each other.[39] Nationally this caused great disquiet and the British Medical Association and the medical press waged what was termed the 'battle of the clubs' from the late 1860s up to the introduction of National Insurance.[40]

Rural branches were also seemingly little concerned with a third type of relief that the affiliated orders saw as a major service for their members: the provision of allowances for unemployed members travelling in search of work. Trade unions had long provided travelling relief and it was a necessary feature of the relief granted by all the main affiliated orders.[41] The rules of the IOOF MU stated that one of its objects was 'for assisting members when compelled to travel in search of employment' and the laws of the Grand United Order of Oddfellows stated more specifically that it had 'the purpose of enabling them [members], when out of employment, to travel in search of work at the expense of the society'.[42] The rules of the GUOOF laid down that any person who had been a member for twelve months and was unemployed, through no fault of his own, could apply for a travelling card which would be issued at the discretion of the lodge or lodge officers. As well as a card the member would be given a number of cheques, previously purchased by the lodge from the national headquarters, which were to be cashed by the district branches in the towns to which the member travelled. The cards were usable for six months. If the member refused any suitable work his card would be stopped.[43] Similar schemes existed in the Independent Order of Oddfellows MU, Ancient Order of Foresters, United Ancient Order of Druids and the National United Order of Free Gardeners. The allowances laid down in the 1878 rules of the NUOFG were one penny per mile between each relieving office plus a bed for not more than fourpence. On Saturday one shilling extra was given and provision for a bed for Sunday night.[44]

There are few references to travelling cards or certificates being granted in the minute books of East Riding village Oddfellows' lodges and Foresters' courts. The Rising Star lodge, IOOF MU,

Beverley, however, granted seven travelling cards in the years 1859-64.[45] A travelling card issued on 25 September 1869 to John Hepton, a smith aged thirty-two, of the Loyal Triumph Lodge, IOOF MU, Beverley, records that he received relief at Beverley on 27 September, Hull on 11 October, Newcastle-on-Tyne on 14 October, North Shields on 15 October, Sunderland, Bishop Wearmouth and Middlesbrough on 16 October, Middlesbrough again the following day, Stockton and Thirsk on 18 October and finally at Malton on the 19 October 1869. He usually received sixpence from each examining officer.[46]

A travelling card ensured that if a member became ill on his journeys or if he died he would receive the benefits to which he was due. In May 1839 a young Oddfellow from Osmotherly, in the North Riding, fell ill and died at Nafferton and as the *Hull Advertiser* recorded:

> A stranger and far from his home, he found brothers with hearts ready to administer relief in the hour of necessity, and funds to administer both to his temporal and spiritual wants; his last remains, when consigned to the silent tomb, were attended by the brothers of Nafferton and Driffield lodge.[47]

The ensuring of a decent burial was one of the principal motives for joining a friendly society and the so called 'funeral benefit' was for many the principal and sometimes only benefit they received in return for many years' contributions. The horror of a pauper funeral led the majority of the working class to make provision in some way to avoid this eventuality. The numerous burial clubs provided more than adequate funeral benefits for a modest monthly subscription or occasional collection on the death of a member. The usual £10 funeral benefit would provide a moderately lavish funeral but the friendly societies, both local and affiliated, provided much more. The subscriber to a burial club may have had the funeral trappings of horse drawn hearse, oak coffin, mutes and the black crepe bedecked undertaker's men but he still could go to the grave virtually unaccompanied but the funeral of a friendly society member would be attended by many of his fellow members who, if belonging to an affiliated order, would wear solemn regalia and go through an elaborate ritual.

The £10 or £12 paid by most affiliated branches on the death of a member and the £6 to £10 on the death of his wife were clearly for defraying 'the expense of the burial' but, when the normal cost of a burial in the mid-late nineteenth century is considered, this sum should also have provided important financial relief for the bereaved.[48] In 1843 the average expense of the funeral of an adult of the 'labouring class' was about £4 and in Hull in 1885 undertakers advertised funerals at £2 18*s* for which a superior hearse, two mourning coaches and a coffin fully trimmed and covered with cloth were provided.[49] In rural areas where there was not the extravagance of the undertakers paraphernalia the costs would have been less. The burial book of a Long Riston joiner records costs ranging from £1 14*s* for the coffin of an elderly widow in 1862 to £15 for the lavish burial of the wife of a wealthy farmer in 1872.[50]

Inadequacies in the friendly society benefits which had not been so evident in the mid-nineteenth century became more apparent in the years 1890-1910 as the number of elderly members rapidly increased and wages rose and, as has been chronicled by Gilbert and Treble, it was this awareness of their precarious financial situation that changed the affiliated order attitudes to state benefits.[51] Generally the strong opposition of the 1890s, mostly voiced against contributory pensions, was changed to qualified support for non-contributory pensions by 1902.

Soon after the passing of the Old Age Pensions Act in 1908 the larger societies realised that it had potentially great advantages for them and provided a basis for ending sickness benefits at seventy. Under the act however the societies lost the concessions gained in 1904 and friendly society benefits were taken into account when calculating an applicant's income for pension purposes. This reversal heightened the desire of the affiliated orders to enter early into the discussions concerning national health insurance which began in the autumn of 1908 straight after the passing of the Old Age Pensions Act. By becoming actively involved in the proposals the affiliated orders hoped to protect their interests but other than being seen from the beginning as an agency through which the national health insurance scheme would be administered, the friendly societies were unsuccessful in securing any distinctive privileges for their members. Their dominant role in the provision of sickness and medical relief was totally undermined by the success of their opponents, the industrial insurance companies and the medical profession, in wresting important concessions from Lloyd George. The indebtedness however of the state schemes of pensions and national insurance to the long established provisions made by the branches of the affiliated orders is clearly indicated by the similarities of the benefits provided.

The state old age pensions when they were introduced were little different to the sickness benefit or 'pensions' granted by affiliated branches to elderly members. The full old age pension available from 1 January 1909 for all aged over seventy years and having an income of less than eight shillings per week was only five shillings, not noticeably more than the 'tiny weekly amount of 4*s* 10*d*' that Pamela Horn records that John Blake of Charlton, Oxfordshire, aged seventy-nine, received from the Oddfellows friendly society in 1903.[52] Similarly the sickness benefits provided under the National Insurance Act from 1913, of 10*s* a week for twenty-six weeks with a reduction then to 5*s* a week, were seemingly based on benefits that had been granted by the affiliated orders for over seventy years. Even the employees weekly contribution of 4*d* to the scheme was the same as the basic contribution of most societies.[53]

For some workers the benefits of national insurance however were not at first as obvious as the benefits of friendly society membership. The introduction of national health insurance was marked by a reduction in wages. Rowntree and Kendall cite the example of the family of an East Riding agricultural labourer, Mr Atkinson, who with wife and five children found themselves 1*s* 7*d* per week worse off from July 1912, a drop of 8 per cent in the family income.[54] From his weekly wage of 19*s*, the farmer docked a shilling to pay the employers contribution and fourpence was taken for the labourers contribution and his wife had to pay threepence a week out of her £4 a year earnings as a school cleaner. Atkinson also paid fourpence a week into a benefit club which, like the majority of his fellow agricultural workers, he had probably done so since he was around eighteen, some twenty-five or more years before. If he kept up his payments he would derive reasonable benefit from his membership but from 1912 there was little incentive for any young agricultural worker to join a friendly society. The whole nature of friendly society benefits changed and an increasingly complex scale of contributions and benefits was introduced which transformed many branches into what were virtually combinations of collecting, deposit and insurance societies as well as being state agencies for health insurance. The man who had joined a village Oddfellows' lodge before 1853 was still able to pay his fourpence a week contribution and receive 10*s* a week sickness benefit and a funeral benefit of £12 but an eighteen year agricultural labourer joining in 1912 had a choice of seventeen basic scales to which he could contribute from 3*d* to 4*s* 9*d* a month in addition to his 4*d* a week for state benefits. If a member continued to pay into his lodge sixpence a week to cover both society and state benefits he could receive, when sick, his state benefit of 10*s* a week for twenty-six weeks plus 2*s* from the society in addition to the death benefit of £12. The sickness benefits ceased at seventy years.[55] From July 1912 the financial benefits of membership of a friendly society became largely supplementary to state benefits and no longer played such an important role in the economic life of the working man.

6

Respectability and Rural Friendly Societies

Friendly societies have generally been regarded as the most reformist and most Victorian value oriented of working-class organisations. Perkin has commented that 'there is no doubt that of all working-class institutions the friendly societies came nearest to the middle-class ideal of self-help and self-dependence'.[1] They were seen by contemporaries as 'prudent and laudable institutions'.[2] The rule books, lecture books and journals of the affiliated orders 'carefully enshrine respectable values' and newspaper reports of their activities stress sobriety and rationality.[3] The friendly society is seen as one of the chief vehicles by which the ethic of respectability was instilled in the working class particularly the upper strata - the artisans. The espousal of respectability by the artisan has been proclaimed as a key factor in the maintenance of social stability in mid-nineteenth century England. By adopting middle-class values the respectable artisan was united with the tradesmen and the employer against what has been termed 'the roughs' - the bulk of the working class.[4]

The precise nature of working-class respectability, its contribution to mid-Victorian reformism and the extent to which it was diffused from above or sought from below have been examined in a number of recent studies.[5] Foster in his study of Oldham propounded a view that in the aftermath of Chartism the labour aristocracy rapidly assimilated middle-class values and attitudes and then began to actively disseminate the culture of their employers and distance themselves from the culture of the mass of workers.[6]

Foster's portrayal of the 'ideological embourgeoisement' of a collaborationist labour aristocracy has however been challenged by writers who have closely examined the artisan elite. Crossick, Gray and Kirk maintain that the Victorian working man's respectability was 'part of an indigenous working-class culture, which was separate from, and largely impervious to, outside attempts to determine its character and direction'.[7] For the working man self-help was best achieved through collective organisations for they provided the means of escape from dependence and deference.[8] The habits of hard-work, thrift and temperance were pursued not because they were imposed from above but because they provided 'practical safeguards against threats of poverty and economic insecurity'.[9]

If the urban affiliated order friendly society was the archetypal institution of the independent artisan through which he assimilated personally beneficial middle-class values into a collective working-class culture, what role did the rural affiliated branch play in a deferential society noticeably lacking an aristocracy of labour? What was the nature of rural working-class respectability as illustrated by the village benefit club? The little that has been written about rural working-class culture at this time would suggest a very different picture. Here the emphasis is on social control and the imposition, by landowners and clergy, of middle-class values and rational activities on a cap-touching dependent labouring class. Is this true? Did the nature of urban and rural working-class respectability differ so markedly?

Mid-Victorian observers of the rural working-class were much troubled by the impact of the affiliated orders for, while commending their encouragement of thrift and self-help, they felt compelled to criticise their close association with public houses and intemperance and their extravagance in ritual and regalia. A correspondent to the Anglican newspaper *The Guardian* in 1862 commented:

> All who are familiar with Friendly Societies know very well that they mean a great deal more than the mere payment of certain premiums and the reception, in time of need, of certain equivalent benefits. They know that they are clubs in another sense of the word also. The name is associated in their minds with

> bands and banners, and processions with scarfs and rosettes, with public-house dinners, and all their natural concomitants. Too often the Club-day in a village means a day of rioting and drunkenness; a day on which respectable people shut up their houses and keep indoors, or take the opportunity of paying a visit to friends at a distance.[10]

The letter goes on to say that although some feast days have 'been seized by an energetic clergyman, and turned into occasions of rational and Christian relaxation' the anniversaries of the affiliated orders with their 'quaint costume, the hieroglyphic banners and long files of members' have defied such personal influence.

Reports of feast days which abound in local newspapers throughout the early summer would however suggest a different picture. There is a tendency to emphasise the involvement of clergy and gentry in the more formal proceedings of the feast day. For example an account of Hunmanby Shepherds' anniversary in 1854 records that after the members had attended the church where they heard 'an excellent discourse delivered by the Rev. R. Mitford Taylor, M.A. . . . they proceeded in a body, colours flying and music playing to the Hall, the residence of Admiral Mitford, who received most kindly their visit, and addressed them at some length, alluding to the seat of war . . . He wished them success in their institution, and having added a donation of two guineas towards their fund, he invited them into the garden.'[11] They afterwards returned to the Swan Inn where their feast was chaired by the rector.

Drawing largely on such newspaper accounts, recent writers have been at pains to portray the feast day as an example of increasing social control of the rural working class. Cunningham has called them 'occasions patronised and controlled by the wealthy and participated in by a deferential populace', and Obelkevich has stressed the self-discipline and deference exhibited by the society members on the day; the orderly processions, moderate drinking, and close involvement of the clergy and farmers all proclaimed their virtue and loyalty.[12] Even 'when they begged contributions from the gentry and farmers they reverted to a comfortingly traditional relationship of paternalism and dependence'.[13] In his study of Whitsun festivities in nineteenth century Oxfordshire, Howkins claims that friendly societies were the decisive influence in 'replacing the wildness of the early years of the century with sobriety and order'. Howkins' writings on friendly societies reverberate with words such as 'control', 'domination', 'taking-over', 'taming', 'reformation', 'organized', and 'monopolized' when discussing the involvement of clergy and gentry.[14] How real was this control and domination? Undoubtedly such positions were sought but how often obtained?

Club feasts in themselves were often far from being occasions of 'rational enjoyment'. Feast days as reported in the newspapers all follow a similar pattern. They begin with the morning gathering of the members at their club room, then the procession with banner, regalia and brass band to the parish church or chapel for the anniversary service, the procession back to the club room for the dinner followed by numerous toasts and speeches and finally a perambulation with the band around the village and neighbourhood. Less space is usually given to the more informal proceedings of the day which involved the whole community. In June 1861 the *Driffield Times* in reporting the twenty-third anniversary of Hutton Cranswick Foresters noted:

> There was a great number of people present and, indeed, it had a great resemblance to a public holiday. Stalls, shooting galleries, and the popular game of Aunt Sally were all more or less patronised throughout the day. The weather was everything that could be desired, and no doubt had a tendency to cause such a large influx of strangers.[15]

Four years later the same newspaper recounts how on the occasion of the anniversary of Nafferton Shepherds' lodge 'The day was kept as a general holiday', with a grand gala in a field behind the King's Head Inn 'where the lovers of racing and other rural sports had an opportunity of enjoying themselves'. There was extensive betting on the 'Nafferton Derby' and several foot races and the day ended with 'some capital clog dancing' and 'dancing on the green to the delightful strains of the Driffield Glee Band'.[16] For these villages and many others the club feast became *the* red letter day of the village calendar and it generally replaced the old village feast as the main festive occasion and was similarly characterised by feasting and drinking and a great gathering of more distant relatives and friends. There may have been orderly processions and modern sideshows and attractions but even in the early twentieth century the feasts were not, as the Yeos have suggested, 'neutered with swings and roundabouts'.[17] Much to the regret of many, including friendly society members and officers, they still exhibited scenes of drunkenness, immorality, and brutality.[18] Throughout the Victorian period the local press and the minute and fine books of affiliated branches carry many references to excessive drinking, fighting and unruly behaviour at club feasts. In June 1840 an inquest was held into the death of a Hutton Cranswick shoemaker who had been killed in a fight after becoming intoxicated at the Oddfellows anniversary at Driffield.[19] That town's Petty Sessions in July 1850 dealt with two men who were charged by a third with threatening his life and it was noted that 'the parties reside at Wetwang and had been drinking at the club feast'.[20] In July 1872 the same court fined four men who were charged with being drunk and disorderly at Cranswick Club Feast.[21] Four years later Cranswick Oddfellows fined a member one shilling 'for being drunk in procession on Feast Day'. The same offence brought fines of five shillings for three members of Middleton Foresters in 1884.[22]

There was little in such feast day celebrations to equate friendly societies with a new more rational culture. Links with intemperance were not confined to the feast days for all but a few friendly societies had their fortnightly or monthly meetings in a room at a pub and such meetings were naturally accompanied by drinking. Nine out of every ten friendly societies in Middlesex in 1845 met in public houses and only one of the eighty-five registered societies in Kentish London between 1855 and 1870 did not.[23] In 1850 352 (96%) of the 366 Foresters' courts in Yorkshire met in pubs and in Lincolnshire 126 (96%) out of 131.[24] Similarly of the 183 East Riding societies founded 1832-74, for which we have an initial meeting place, 169 (92%) met in a public house.[25] Anglican clergy and the Methodist hierarchy were vehement in their condemnation of this close association of club and alehouse. Clergy testifying to a committee on intemperance set up by the Convocation of York in 1874 saw it as a major cause of village drunkenness. One cleric reported: 'I have, in six years, attended the death-beds of, I think, seven men, whose deaths were caused by drink, and their drinking habits mainly by their clubs.'[26]

There was strong pressure from the clergy for friendly societies to remove to the church schoolroom or village reading room and every encouragement was given to clubs which opened their own halls. However despite such pressure and the strong Methodist connections of many of the societies' officers the majority of East Riding clubs still met at village public houses in 1900 and had not yet achieved true Victorian respectability which according to Brian Harrison 'required shunning the pub'.[27]

It was not only in their feast days and public house meetings that friendly societies retained what Bailey describes as 'the obsolescent survivals of an older and intemperate way of life, the hangovers from a semi-barbarous folk culture', but also in their ritual, regalia and semi-secrecy.[28] The trappings of freemasonry which were adopted by the affiliated branches might seem to have more association with the rationality of the eighteenth century enlightenment than the folk-culture of rural England but parallels abound. The wearing of sashes, costumes and other regalia and the processions with music to the chief houses of the neighbourhood seeking donations which characterised feast days had marked similarities to the ritual of Plough Monday which was generally disappearing in the East Riding in the 1830s.[29] On that day 'plough boys' dressed up in fantastic costumes and accompanied by music went around the larger houses begging subscriptions and performing a ritualised play. The secrecy and ritual of the affiliated orders had its parallel in the secret societies of horsemen, recorded in East Anglia by George Ewart Evans and north-east Scotland by Ian Carter, an organisation that is also likely to have existed in the East Riding.[30]

The funerals of affiliated order members were great public spectacles in the early days of the societies and aroused wide interest and criticism. In July 1839 more than 1000 spectators saw a young shoemaker buried at Ruston Parva accompanied by 200 of his fellow Foresters in their regalia. Music was provided by three trumpeters and a 'solemn and impressive' oration was given by a member from Hull.[31] The following year 600 people accompanied the body of an Oddfellow four miles from North Frodingham to his funeral at Skipsea and no less than 4000 assembled at Bridlington to see the funeral procession of a leading Rechabite.[32] A fuller account of a funeral of an Oddfellow at Louth, Lincolnshire in 1846 indicates the features that incensed Anglican clergy and others. A procession of 140 Oddfellows wearing their 'usual paraphernalia' was headed by two men carrying large naked swords, followed by another carrying an hour glass on an open bible. The coffin was draped with the deceased's sash and apron. After a church service a funeral oration was given by an Oddfellow, who was also a Methodist local preacher, two verses of a hymn were sung and then each Oddfellow threw into the grave a sprig of thyme.[33] Such 'ludicrous' and 'grotesque' ceremonies were roundly condemned and seen as likely 'to revive ancient heathenism and to plunge those who live in the nineteenth century into all the ignorance and barbarism of Pagan Britain'.[34]

Despite the presence of clergy and gentry at feast days and their obvious concern over the activities of the affiliated orders there is little sign that they had any real success in imposing their views upon the membership. Minute books of East Riding affiliated branches show that the control of the societies remained firmly with the members. Clergy often gave donations, they were sometimes members, and sometimes they held office but always the decisions were made by the membership. In January 1888 Lockington Foresters received a letter signed by five local Anglican clergy, including two honorary members, asking if their feast day could be removed from a Friday for religious reasons. The Foresters took a vote, two were for the change and forty-five against.[35] Similarly the decisions about the venue for the anniversary service and the preacher were made without consulting the incumbent. During the first twenty-five years of its existence the Foresters' court at Hutton Cranswick invariably attended the parish church but only occasionally was the vicar the preacher. On at least twelve occasions the choice of preacher was voted upon and although each time the vicar, Mr Rigby, was nominated he only came top of the poll five times.[36] The invitations to preach were sent out once the result was known and it must have been chastening for the incumbent to find himself supplanted in his own church at so many anniversaries. He may however have been pleased to be spared the duty of preaching to what was seemingly often an inattentive congregation and clearly he was financially better off. For not only was the preacher not paid but he was expected to make a donation to the club funds.[37]

The use of the parish church for anniversary services was established practice for the local societies founded in the late eighteenth and early nineteenth centuries and this tradition was carried on by the majority of the affiliated branches.[38] There was however neither any sign of deference nor religious partisanship in the choice. The church was the traditional place for village meetings and its neutrality and long established secular role made it the most acceptable venue for the bulk of the membership. The East Riding villager would undoubtedly have agreed with the Stockport Chartists who in 1839 repeatedly insisted that 'The church was unquestionably the property of the public'.[39] In 1849 the members of Bainton Shepherds lodge were somewhat offended when they had to apply to eight Anglican clergy before finding one who would officiate for them, 'it being their invariable custom to have a sermon preached to them at the parish church'.[40] Affiliated branches were sometimes forced to hold their service elsewhere. The newly formed Foresters court at Kilham was refused the use of the church by the curate in 1839 and therefore held its service at the Baptist chapel and in 1841 a similar refusal led Welton Foresters to hold their anniversary service at the Wesleyan chapel.[41]

On these occasions the attendance at an Anglican church was the first choice but this was not always so. In the years 1839-46 there are reports of the attendance of Leven Foresters, Wetwang and Nafferton Shepherds and Brandesburton and Driffield Oddfellows at Wesleyan chapels, Newport and Keyingham Foresters and Driffield Rechabites at Primitive Methodist chapels and Cottingham Foresters and Bridlington Druids at Independent chapels.[42] Later in the century the Oddfellows and Foresters at Hutton Cranswick on occasion chose a chapel rather than the parish church for their service. The Foresters minute book records that in 1875 the service was held at the Primitive Methodist chapel and the following year a proposition that the Primitive Methodist minister be invited to preach was carried by thirteen votes. In 1877 however the voting was: parish church twenty-two, Baptist chapel five, and Primitive Methodist chapel four. Eleven years later the ballot resulted in a dead heat with the Primitive Methodist chapel getting twenty-one votes and the parish church twenty-one.[43]

Obelkevich's statement concerning friendly societies in South Lindsey that 'they always chose the parish church for their anniversaries' was not applicable in the East Riding and similarly his view that the not infrequent naming of courts and lodges after the principal landowners was a sign of deference needs also to be questioned.[44] In the East Riding the Sykes, Leconfield, Wenlock, Bethel, St. Quintin, Middleton, and Hotham families, amongst others, had courts and lodges named after them. The practice was by no means confined to closed or estate villages for there was a Court Hotham at Hutton Cranswick and a Court St. Quintin at the open village of Rillington. The landowner's name was principally used to give an aura of respectability to the newly formed society in the same way that the orders' names, harking back to antiquity, sought to suggest stability and in both cases the recruitment of members was the chief object. Financial support from landowners was clearly also an aim and this was emphasised by the annual visits made by the societies on their feast days to their residences if nearby. Their annual donations and those of other honorary members of 10*s*, a guinea, or more, provided welcome additions to the funds. If there was deference it was calculated deference employed, as with the practice of respectability described by Peter Bailey, in order 'to extract material and social benefits from class superiors'.[45]

As the century progressed the role was reversed and it was increasingly class superiors who sought benefits from association with friendly societies. The new breed of resident and socially conscious Anglican clergy that spread into the countryside in the late Victorian period saw involvement with, rather than control of, the village club as one way of reaching the bulk of their dissenting or indifferent parishioners.[46] Clergy such as the Revd W.A. Pearman, vicar of Bishop Burton 1888-1923, found themselves actively encouraging the continuance of the feast days and attending the public house meetings.[47] This was a far cry from the writer in *The Guardian* thirty-five years before who had hoped that 'by degrees the feasts and processions will sink more into the background' or the contemporary Lincolnshire clergyman who strongly condemned 'The half-heathen clubs [which are] utterly unlawful for a Christian man'.[48]

The ritual, regalia and intemperance were hardly more acceptable but affiliated societies had achieved such dominance as *the* most representative organisation of the working man that they could neither be ignored nor effectively controlled. In addition the passing of the Reform Act in 1884 and the enfranchisement of the rural working class gave the village clubs great political significance and this has not yet been noted by political historians.[49] The annual feasts provided great gatherings of the new voters, and politicians, both local and national, vied with each other to attend and speak on these occasions. The clergy were joined on the high table by Members of Parliament, prospective candidates, political agents and, after 1889, by county councillors. Numbers of honorary members similarly increased but few could equal the total of 41 honorary members amassed by the Garden of Eden lodge of the National United Order of Free Gardeners at Driffield by 1912. This impressive total included tradesmen, doctors, solicitors, clergy, Hull Brewery Company and two Members of Parliament.[50] The two M.Ps., Sir Luke White and Mark Sykes, were probably the politicians who most actively cultivated the friendly society interest in the East Riding in the years before the First World War. White, a nonconformist Driffield solicitor with working-class origins, was the Liberal agent, 1892-1900, and then M.P. for the Buckrose division, 1900-18, and Sykes, a Roman Catholic and the heir to the largest East Riding landed estate, was the Unionist candidate for the division 1907-11.[51] During this last period the two men were invited to and attended large numbers of club feasts throughout the Wolds and adjoining area. In 1909 Sykes accepted invitations to twenty-two feasts and attended seventeen.[52] White, as the sitting member, was more restricted in his attendance but the importance which he attached to them is evidenced by the lengths which he took to get to them. On one occasion he reached Middleton church just in time for the morning feast-day service, having taken part in a division at the House of Commons at midnight.[53] This frantic canvassing of village clubs illustrates the dominant role that friendly societies had come to play in rural society. The regular reports in Anglican parish magazines in the early twentieth century clearly demonstrate how respectable the 'ungodly associations' had become.

The respectability that had been achieved was not a product of social control by landowner and parson but it had been achieved by the members on their own terms. Urban and rural working-class respectability did not differ; they were both very much part of an indigenous independent culture. The approval and financial support of other classes was welcomed but there was great hostility to any form of direct control and subordination.[54] As with the urban labour aristocracy the rural working class 'plundered middle-class culture for products to mould into their own traditions'.[55] The self-discipline necessarily assumed for the successful involvement in a complex financial organisation did not mean a total displacement of features of a traditional culture. Peter Bailey has pointed out the anomalies present in friendly societies and suggests that to the members these were normalities and that the 'concurrent pursuit of "thinking and drinking", "virtue and vice" represented not so much a conflict of value systems as a reconciliation'.[56] A reconciliation determined by the working-classes and not the middle-classes. The dominated and deferential village club is an illusion of recent writers and does a great disservice to an institution which more than any other in the Victorian countryside produced an authentic and widespread working-class culture.

Conclusion

The foregoing study is offered as a contribution both to the necessary reassessment of the role of friendly societies in Victorian England and to the history of the rural working-class. Although confined to an examination of affiliated order friendly societies in one purely agricultural county, it has been shown conclusively that many of the accepted generalisations about friendly societies are inaccurate. No longer can the societies be dismissed as being the preserve of the respectable urban artisan nor can the benefits that members received be considered as insignificant. There is little sign in the East Riding that the village societies were controlled by the wealthy or that the membership was deferential. The societies thrived in the larger independent open settlements where they acted as the major unifying factor for a working class generally divided into communities centred around the chapels and alehouses. Through the activities of the societies, particularly in the monthly meetings and annual feast days, the traditional way of life represented by communal activities, ritual, superstition and intemperate conviviality was combined with the new values of self-improvement and respectability to produce a clearly distinguishable rural working-class culture in the second half of the nineteenth century.[1]

There are indications that friendly societies are about to be 'discovered', for the number of books and articles coming out that give them more than a passing mention is increasing, yet the surprising neglect commented on by Eric Hobsbawm thirty years ago is still apparent among labour historians. Alun Howkins in his recent work *Poor Labouring Men: rural radicalism in Norfolk 1870-1923* confines his discussion of friendly societies to two pages concerned with one untypical society and to a photograph with the caption 'Radicalism: the friendly society ... Many of the early unionists of the 1870s and 1880s cut their teeth in friendly societies', yet within Howkins' area of study there were numerous branches of the Oddfellows and Foresters and some of the key figures in the study were active officers in them.[2] Here neglect is not through ignorance but choice and it can be only assumed that Howkins, along with many others, dismisses the relevance of friendly societies to the labour movement.

In his account of York in the first half of the nineteenth century Armstrong claims that the 'ethos of individualism and self-help, and tendency to social exclusiveness' exhibited in friendly societies meant that they 'must be regarded as only very tenuously associated with the labour movement'.[3] This present study has shown that the labels of 'individualism' and 'self-help' should be replaced by 'collectivism' and 'mutual-aid' and there is little sign of 'social exclusiveness' in the societies that have been examined. Links with the labour movement as represented by trade unionism and co-operatives are not apparent in the rural East Riding but a limited search through secondary sources suggests that elsewhere they are considerable.

The rise of the affiliated orders in the period 1830-50 was on a par with other working class movements and many a Chartist, trade-unionist or co-operator was an active friendly society member. Kirk gives a number of examples from Lancashire including William Marcroft a leading figure in the co-operative movement at Oldham who had been a Chartist, an Oddfellow, a Rechabite and a member of the Machine Grinders' Society.[4] Many more such men figure in the pages of Joyce Bellamy and John Saville's *Dictionary of Labour Biography* including the following: James Daly, Owenite, Rochdale Pioneer and a prominent member of the Oddfellows society; James Lees, Oldham co-operative pioneer and court and district secretary of the Foresters for over 30 years; and Thomas Piggott, the ironworkers' leader in the Black Country, secretary for many years of both a court of the Ancient Order of Foresters and a lodge of the Order of United Free Gardeners. Numerous miners' leaders including Enoch Edwards, Fred Hall, Levi Lovett, Willy Lunn and Herbert Smith were life-long active members of affiliated societies.[5] Frequently membership and office-holding in a friendly society precedes active involvement in a trade union.

The affiliated orders experienced their greatest expansion during the period of Chartist agitation and it would be surprising if there were not links between the movements. Oddfellows' lodges were a source of finance for Chartists in the Newport Rising in 1839, and their ceremonial swords were used in the conflict.[6] At Bradford and Barnsley the Oddfellows' Halls were used for Chartist meetings and when Ben Rushton, a leading Halifax Chartist, was buried, in 1853, his coffin was escorted by 140 Oddfellows.[7] The *Northern Star*, the Chartist newspaper, carried reports on the opening of friendly society branches and members' funerals, as well as articles on the orders.[8]

Such links with labour movements in the 1830s-40s are amongst the many aspects of friendly societies that have yet to be explored. This study has touched on one limited rural area but has demonstrated something of what can be learnt from the surprising wealth of original sources that exist. In Appendix B a brief account of the primary sources for a regional study of friendly societies is given. There is an urgent need for the location, preservation and study of the friendly society records throughout Britain. Currently too many of these records are being destroyed as branch after branch of the affiliated orders is being closed down or amalgamated. Although the great majority of surviving documents are still with the present, or former, branch officers, an increasing number of branch archives are to be found in record offices and are readily accessible for research. There can be no justification for historians of the urban and rural working class to continue to neglect friendly societies. They constituted the largest, most representative, and possibly best documented, working-class organisation to develop in Victorian Britain.

Appendix A: Origins and Early Development of the Chief Affiliated Orders

The early history of most of the orders is obscure despite the large number of Order histories that were produced in the late nineteenth and early twentieth centuries. T.B. Stead's *A Short History of the Chief Affiliated Friendly Societies*, Leeds, 1880, which he published anonymously is the only contemporary work which provides authoritative accounts of the early history of the main orders. The following section gives brief details on the origin and development of the chief affiliated orders that had a significant membership in the East Riding.[1]

Independent Order of Oddfellows, Manchester Unity

In the 1880s there were at least thirty separate orders of Oddfellows in England. All these orders could trace their origins, directly or indirectly, back to convivial societies existing in London in the mid-eighteenth century.[2] The first authentic reference to an Oddfellows' society relates to the Aristarchus lodge of Oddfellows which was meeting at the Globe Tavern, Hatton Garden, London in 1748.[3] In the second half of the century London Oddfellows' clubs were grouped into two 'orders', the Ancient and the Patriotic. Around 1779 these amalgamated to form the United Order of Oddfellows and by 1796 there was also a Grand Independent Order of Oddfellows in London. Both orders had opened dependent lodges in various parts of England by the end of the century. In 1804 the Grand Lodge of the United

Order of Oddfellows was dissolved and the provincial branches became independent lodges paving the way for the establishment of affiliated orders in the second decade of the century.[4] The exact date when the various Oddfellows' orders and lodges moved from being convivial societies to fully fledged friendly or benefit societies is unclear; the first seemingly being the Independent Order of Oddfellows, Manchester Unity, (IOOF MU) in 1823.

The founding lodge of the IOOF MU was the Abercromby Lodge opened at Manchester 10 October 1810. In 1813 the Abercromby lodge, the Victory lodge and others from the area held a meeting to establish a common funeral fund and assumed the title of the Independent Order of Oddfellows under the Manchester Compliance. The following year the order began corresponding with Oddfellows lodges all over the country inviting co-operation. At Whitsun 1822, by which time dispensations had been granted to 100 lodges, the words 'Manchester Unity' were substituted for 'Manchester Compliance' in the title of the order. Although still primarily a convivial society, funeral gifts and other benevolent grants were an increasing feature of the lodges' work and the revised laws of 1823 required every member to contribute threepence per week to finance the benefits.[5] The order was remarkably successful and by 1834 it had 781 lodges and 47,638 members. In 1842 the Order claimed to consist of upwards of 3500 lodges and about 220,000 members but three years later it suffered a major set back when 16,000 members left the order and formed the National Independent Order of Oddfellows.[6] It was not until after 1853 that the IOOF MU once again began to expand to become, what it claimed to be in the 1890s, 'the richest [friendly society] in the world'.[7]

Grand United Order of Oddfellows

In the later 19th century the second largest Oddfellows' order was the Grand United Order of Oddfellows (GUOOF) which claimed to be of greater antiquity than the Manchester Unity. In 1810, six years after the dissolution of the London Grand Lodge of the United Order of Oddfellows, three former Sheffield lodges of the order met to discuss bringing themselves 'under the bond of Union'.[8] This seemingly resulted in the formation of the Sheffield Grand Lodge which steadily expanded in the industrial areas of Yorkshire and Lancashire and in

1833 issued a list of some 100 lodges under its authority.[9] Following internal disputes the lodges formed themselves in 1837 into the Grand United Order of Oddfellows and the headquarters moved to Leeds.[10] From this date the order became more clearly a benefit society.

In common with all the affiliated orders the GUOOF experienced periods of agitation and disaffection but its more democratic government seems to have prevented any major split.[11] The order developed a major following in America and Australia and in 1912 the UK membership was only 85,575 out of a total adult male membership of 430,817.[12]

The Ancient Order of Foresters

The existence of Court No.1 of the Order of Royal Foresters meeting at the Old Crown Inn, Kirkgate, Leeds in 1790 seems to be the first authentic information on the Foresters.[13] In 1813 a second court was opened at Harrogate and by 1834 there were 358 courts of which 203 were in Yorkshire and 119 in Lancashire.[14] In August 1834 a dispute over the autocratic control of the initial Leeds court led to the majority of the courts breaking away and forming the Ancient Order of Foresters (AOF) which was immediately successful and four years later its 1001st court was opened and this rapid expansion continued until 1847-9 when severe economic depression and internal disputes led to a decrease in lodges and membership.[15] Recruitment revived in 1850 and the order spread rapidly to southern and eastern England. There was no further set back until the late 1880s by which time the Foresters had overtaken the IOOFMU in membership but not in funds.[16]

United Ancient Order of Druids

The various orders of Druids are traditionally considered to have originated with a convivial society established at the King's Arms Tavern, Poland Street, London on 21 November 1781. Druids lodges were opened throughout the country reaching the north by the 1820s. Following disputes over moves to become a benefit society the United Ancient Order of Druids (UAOD) was formed on 26 December 1833 when representatives of fifty-three disaffected lodges of the Ancient

Order of Druids met at the Crown Tavern, Clerkenwell Green. The control and support of the new order was chiefly in the North and the Midlands. In 1858 a majority of the lodges seceded and formed the Order of Druids.[17]

The Order of Druids drew its greatest support from Lancashire and Yorkshire and in 1864 could boast 804 lodges and 41,609 members in England and Wales while the United Ancient Order of Druids, after some recovery, had only 221 lodges in 1861 and 17,828 members in 1867.[18] The numerical superiority of the secessionists continued into the 1870s. However in the later nineteenth century the UAOD expanded greatly and in 1914 it had 179,966 members compared to the Order of Druids' 70,486 members.[19]

Loyal Order of Ancient Shepherds, Ashton Unity

The origins, establishment and subsequent history of the Loyal Order of Ancient Shepherds (LOAS) are more fully recorded than for most of the other affiliated orders. On Christmas Day 1826 twelve men met at the Friendship Inn, Old Street, Ashton-under-Lyne, for the purpose of setting up a new benefit society. The landlord, Thomas Scholfield, was an Oddfellow and it had been the original intention of those meeting to form a lodge of the IOOF MU. However their application to open a lodge had been refused and thus they resolved to form an independent society 'The Society of Ancient Shepherds'.

A second lodge was opened, in October 1827, at Mossley and the development of the order had begun. Ten years after the founding of the order it consisted of thirteen districts and 176 lodges almost all in Lancashire and the West Riding of Yorkshire and by 1848 there were 524 lodges and 15,155 members. In that year the Wisbech district seceded and membership dropped by 1384. A further decrease occurred in 1850 but from the following year the pattern was of a steady increase in membership particularly after 1870.[20]

National United Order of Free Gardeners

Although a number of Orders of Gardeners existed in England in the nineteenth century, only one, the National United Order of Free

Gardeners (NUOFG), was of national importance.[21] The society is said to have been founded in the neighbourhood of Oldham in about 1820. By 1840 the Order, then known as the Order of Ancient Free Gardeners, Lancashire Union, had opened some 500 lodges chiefly in Lancashire and the West and North Ridings. A split occurred in 1842 and the Leeds, York, Knaresborough, Harrogate, Sheffield, Birmingham and Hayfield districts seceded to form an order called The Order of Ancient Free Gardeners, Yorkshire Union. The Lancashire Union which was renamed The United Order of Free Gardeners still retained many Yorkshire lodges and rapidly built up a dominant position. The Yorkshire Union or Unity which was renamed The Grand National Order of Free Gardeners in 1848 did not have such success and in 1871 it amalgamated with the United Order of Free Gardeners. The order added the word National to its title when it registered under the Friendly Societies Act of 1875.[22]

Independent Order of Rechabites, Salford Unity

In 1835 the Committee of the Manchester and Salford Temperance Society established the Salford Temperance Burial Society which later that year became No.1 Ebenezer Tent, Independent Order of Rechabites (IOR). In November 1835 a second tent was opened in Salford and during 1836 a further thirty-nine tents were opened chiefly in north-west England. Within ten years 1112 tents had been opened.

In 1836, because of the pressure for opening the tents to women, there was established the United Order of Female Rechabites (UOFR). The early female tents were all in Yorkshire. The expansion of the female order seems to have come to an abrupt halt in July 1843 by which time 369 tents had been opened. A speedy decline followed and the remnants of the order were united with the IOR in August 1856.

The decline that hit the UOFR was part of the catastrophic reversal in fortune that beset the Rechabites generally. Nationally membership dropped from the 26,000 returned for January 1843 to less than 6000 in 1856. Membership remained around 6000 until 1863 when the order once again began to expand and it rapidly regained its position amongst the leading affiliated orders.[23]

Order of the Sons of Temperance

The Order of the Sons of Temperance (OST) was the last of the major affiliated orders to be established and the only one that was not English in origin. This American Order, founded in New York in 1842, forbade its members to 'make, buy, sell, or use, as a beverage, any spirituous or malt liquor, wine or cider' and prohibited them 'from manufacturing, purchasing, or selling all alcoholic or intoxicating liquors'.[24] The order was introduced into England at Liverpool in 1849. The lodges of the Order are called Sub[ordinate] Divisions, the districts Grand Divisions and the annual meetings National Divisions. By 1878, when the order had become totally independent of the American order, it was well established in the industrial areas of the North and Midlands as well as in South Wales, Glasgow and London.[25] By 1872 the order had 11,625 members and it rapidly expanded at the end of the century and along with the Rechabites, in contrast to the non-temperance orders, it experienced a meteoric rise at the beginning of the twentieth century.[26]

Table 18 : Affiliated Order Membership 1845-1912

	IOOF MU	AOF	LOAS	NUOFG	GUOOF	UAOD	IOR	OST
1845	248526	76990	14169 a	-	31023	-	26000	-
1850	224090	84348	14636	14977	37000 b	-	9060	-
1855	239783	109102	17690	-	-	-	5940 c	-
1860	305241	189584	23477	19522	-	-	6115	-
1865	373509	301077	30844	20559	62206 d	-	-	-
1870	434100	376663	32875	27782	71107	19317 e	15402	11625 e
1875	496529	491196	56053	40834	-	-	-	-
1880	532520	555062	61246	37756	-	22172 f	34641	14021 f
1885	*550729	*594921	66941	45795	-	27550	67722	22122
1890	*594868	*639738	88883	52061	171092 g	31994	95074	26663
1895	*665233	*654233	107525	55515	-	39732	*103045	34894
1900	*736181	*6663232	118338	61623	*78077	47261	*137316	49287
1905	*754239	*651681	125921	58803	*73798	54341	*175639	82235
1910	*749363	*605971	121803	51785	*69898	53248	*213352	97262
1912	*752937	*655882	145691	54718	*85575	62895	*226824	113838

*UK membership only

Figures for alternative years a.1846; b.1851; c.1856; d.1864; e.1872; f.1878; g.1889

Sources: IOOF MU 1845-80 C. Hardwick, *The History, Present Position and Social Importance of Friendly Societies*, 3rd edn, (London, 1893) pp.24-25; AOF 1845-1880 T.B.Stead, *Directory of the Ancient Order of Foresters' Friendly Society for 1896* (Dundee, 1896) pp.621,624; LOAS D.H. Hague, *Historical Sketch of The Loyal Order of Ancient Shepherds* (Stockport, c. 1967) pp.33-34; NUOFG 1850-90 NUOFG Annual Returns 1851, 1857-90; GUOOF J. Thornley, *History of the Grand United Order of Oddfellows* pt.II (Manchester, 1913) p.95; C. Hardwick, p.26; T.B. Stead, *A Short History of the Chief Affiliated Orders* (Leeds, 1880) p.24; J.F.Wilkinson, *Mutual Thrift*, p.160; UAOD T.B.Stead, pp.61; Royal Commission on Friendly Societies PP 1874, [c.996] XXIII Pt.II p.24; IOR R.Highet, *Rechabite History*, Manchester, 1936 p.501; OST T.B. Stead, p.102; J.F.Wilkinson, p.161; All except GUOOF 1886-1895 6th Annual Abstract of Labour Statistics PP 1900 [Cd.119) 1xxxiii, pp.52-53; All 1900-1912 16th Abstract of Labour Statistics PP 1914 [Cd.7131] 1xxx, p.266.

Appendix B: Primary Sources for a Regional Study of Friendly Societies

1. Manuscript Records of Individual Societies, Lodges and Courts

Records of individual friendly societies are to be found in record offices, libraries and museums but the greater part of the surviving documentary material still remains in the hands of local lodges and courts of the affiliated orders and this is under constant threat of destruction or dispersal as more and more independent branches close or come under district supervision.[1] The unearthing of these records depends primarily on personal contact with branch and district secretaries whose names can be sought from the national headquarters of the orders. Letters to branch secretaries rarely, if ever, produce a reply yet telephone calls and personal visits usually reveal some original material - it can be disappointing and consist of a single early twentieth century minute book or if lucky almost all the possible records and regalia going back to the founding of the society in the late 1830s.[2] The amount of material surviving for a branch of an affiliated order, which may have been in existence for almost 150 years, can be vast in quantity and range. The following categories of records however are the most useful:[3]

a. *Minute books*

The content of minute books varies greatly but generally the following items are included. The election and appointment of officers. Acceptance and expulsion of members. Records of fines. Disputes over the behaviour of members and sickness and death benefits. Appointment of club doctor. Discussions about annual feasts and the choice of venue, preacher and band. Purchase and use of regalia. Amendments of lodge and district laws. Investment of funds and details of mortgages. Granting of clearances and travelling cards.

b. *Proposition books*

These are the most valuable source of information on the occupation, residence and age of members on joining the society. In the case of the IOOF MU and AOF printed proposition books are usually used.

c. *Registers of members*

On certain occasions societies produced full registers of their membership. These are usually of the late nineteenth or early twentieth centuries and can give details of name; address; age; occupation; marriage; date of admission; date and reason for termination of membership; if by death, cause of death given; and contributions.

d. *Contribution books*

The record of the weekly, monthly or quarterly payments by members of their subscriptions. Generally a new list of members and their contributions is begun each year so the books provide an invaluable record of fluctuations in membership. The most useful series of contribution books so far located are those for Court Friendship, Ancient Order of Foresters, at Keyingham, North Humberside, which run from 1858 to 1920. In these a new list of members is given each year with the current known address and the movements of members over a sixty year period can be traced.

e. *Account and cash books*

Numerous account and cash books survive for all aspects of friendly society work. Treasurers' general account books recording the societies' income from members, honorary members, and investments and expenditure on sickness and death benefits. Cash books relating to expenditure on the annual feast and lodge room or hall. Benefit stewards' account books recording out-payments and the societies' doctors' accounts.

f. *Sickness registers*

Lists of members with columns recording sickness benefit paid each year or lists of only those who received benefit.

2. Rule Books

The printed or manuscript rules of local societies and courts and lodges of the affiliated orders are the type of friendly society record most widely available and the one that has most often been used in local and regional studies. The majority of surviving rules are for societies which registered with the Clerk of the Peace for the county after 1793, or with the Registrar of Friendly Societies after 1846. Some, but not all, of the rules which were registered with the Clerk of the Peace were transferred to the Registry of Friendly Societies after 1854. The rules of registered societies are to be found in the following places:

a. *Quarter sessions records*

Now usually in the appropriate county record office.

b. *Public Record Office, Kew*

The largest collection of friendly society rules is in the Public Record Office. Following the Public Records Act of 1958 the following records were transferred from the Registry of Friendly Societies:

i. All surviving documents (i.e. rules and amendments of rules) of societies registered and subsequently removed from the register before 1914.

ii. All surviving documents of societies removed from the register after 1913 which were registered before 1875.

iii. A 10% sample of other societies removed from the register after 1913.[4]

c. *Registry of Friendly Societies*

The rules of registered friendly societies which are still functioning are kept in the Registry of Friendly Societies, London.

d. *Miscellaneous collections*

The rules of registered and non-registered friendly societies are to be found in many libraries and record offices as well as private collections.[5]

3. Records of the Affiliated Orders

The principal collections at the order headquarters are mainly printed works with little surviving in manuscript form. In most cases the minutes of the executive committees or boards were printed and circulated quarterly and annually and therefore manuscript minute and account books have only been kept in a few cases.[6] The most useful national sources are:

a. *Dispensation books*

In the case of three orders, AOF, LOAS and GUOOF, the manuscript dispensation books survive and these record the date when courts and lodges were first granted permission to open, and their number, name and meeting place. The AOF and GUOOF granted dispensations and the LOAS surances.

b. *Quarterly and annual reports*

The AOF have preserved their printed quarterly reports from 1834 and the IOOF MU theirs from 1839. The reports contain the minutes of the executive committees, accounts, details of the lodges and courts opened during the quarter and information on action taken against defaulting members and branches.[7]

c. *Directories*

Each order at some date began to produce annual lists of their lodges and courts but except for the AOF they have been poorly preserved. The AOF is said to have published its first *Directory* in 1835, but the earliest consulted was produced in 1840 with a supplement three years later. The full run of annual directories at the AOF headquarters begins in 1845 to the present, with only a gap in 1855. The earliest *List of Lodges* at the IOOF MU headquarters is as late as 1860 although Gosden reproduces pages from a list of 1836, and lists of 1845 and 1850 have been located elsewhere.[8]

The earliest lists and directories usually give number, name and meeting place of each lodge or court arranged by county, and also number of members. By the end of the century the information provided is quite extensive. For instance in the 1896 AOF directory the following are amongst the details given for each court: number; name; year founded; meeting place; frequency of meetings; meeting nights; name and address of secretary; name of treasurer; average rate of interest per cent realised by the court upon investment of its funds; number of benefit members; average age of members; number of honorary members; worth of court funds; days sickness paid for during the year; number of members initiated; number of members died; number of members left through non-payment of contributions; number of wives and widows died; number of members paying contributions graduated according to age; the year when the last valuation of the assets and liabilities was made; and whether or not the court is registered as a branch or society.

d. *Order magazines*

In the 1830s-40s most of the affiliated orders began producing their own journals both to disseminate information about the orders and to advance their cause by underlining their respectability and commitment to the intellectual as well as financial improvement of their members.

The IOOF MU was the first to have a magazine *The Odd Fellows' Magazine* which began as a quarterly journal in March 1828. A nearly complete set is at the IOOF MU headquarters. The AOF *Foresters' Miscellany* began in March 1836 but there were years when it was not produced. The AOF have copies for 1841-43 and 1858 to the present. The IOR have some early copies, 1840-45, of *The Rechabite and Temperance Magazine*, and the NUOFG copies of their journal from October 1879.

4. Parliamentary Papers

Official sources for the study of friendly societies were extensively used by Gosden and a full list of relevant Parliamentary papers is given in his *Friendly societies* pp.248-250. The following were found particularly useful in this regional study:

a. *Annual reports of the Registrar (from 1876 the Chief Registrar) of Friendly Societies in England and Wales 1856-1920.*

The amount of material to be discovered in these annual reports, which record membership and financial details of those registered societies who had made returns, is immense but it has to be treated with caution. All sorts of mistakes have crept into the printed returns, societies have been wrongly named; placed in the wrong village, town or county; figures for one society have been transposed with those of another; courts or lodges of affiliated orders are listed as independent societies or vice versa; and non-existent societies have been created. Notwithstanding all their shortcomings, the reports do provide vital information unobtainable elsewhere.

b *Abstracts of answers and returns relative to the expense and maintenance of the poor in England 1803-4 and 1818.*

c. *Reports of the Royal Commission appointed to enquire into Friendly and Benefit Building Societies 1871-74.*

d. *Reports of the Royal Commission on Labour 1892-94.*

e. *Reports of the Royal Commission on the Aged Poor 1895.*

f. *Reports of the Royal Commission on the Poor Law 1909.*

5. Newspapers and Parish Magazines

Where no documentary material survives the principal sources of information on individual societies in the 19th century are local newspapers and parish magazines.

Above all it is the reports of the anniversaries of the societies that begin to fill the local news columns by the mid-19th century. The editor of the *Driffield Times* commented in June 1874:

> We are rather apprehensive that the reports of friendly societies' anniversaries or club feasts, as they are called, have lately been so frequently inserted in the public prints of the neighbourhood, that the publishing of many more might almost appear to be a monopoly of the press, and that readers might be led to conclude that the space they occupy might be filled with more useful matter.[9]

The value of local newspapers and the extent of information they provide is admirably shown in Rex Russell's study of North Lincolnshire friendly societies.[10]

6. Miscellaneous Sources

Valuable material on friendly societies can be found in a vast array of miscellaneous sources including school log books; trade directories; diaries; parish records and clerical account books. Local topographical works sometimes list friendly societies and give date of foundation and membership.

Notes

Notes for pages 1-4

Introduction

1. This study is based on D. Neave, 'Friendly Societies in the Rural East Riding 1830-1912', Ph.D. thesis, Hull, 1986. I would like to thank my supervisor John Saville for his encouragement and patience during the preparation of both my thesis and this monograph. I wish also to express my thanks for the help and advice provided by my wife Susan Neave, and Dr Joyce Bellamy and Miss Jean Smith of Hull University Press.
2. Neave, thesis, pp. 417-19; J.F. Wilkinson, *Mutual Thrift* (London, 1891) p. 191.
3. E.J. Hobsbawm and G. Rudé, *Captain Swing* (Harmondsworth, 1973) p. 255; J. Foster, *Class Struggle and the Industrial Revolution* (London, 1977) p. 216; G. Crossick, *An Artisan Elite in Victorian Society* (London, 1978) p. 174; A. Armstrong, *Stability and Change in an English County Town - A Social Study of York* (Cambridge, 1974) p. 65.
4. E. Hobsbawm, 'Friendly Societies', *Amateur Historian*, 3, 1957, 98-9.
5. P.H.J.H. Gosden, *The Friendly Societies in England 1815-1875* (Manchester, 1961); see also idem, *Self-Help: voluntary associations in nineteenth-century Britain* (London, 1973).
6. E.P. Thompson, *The Making of the English Working Class* (Harmondsworth, 1968) pp. 457-61.
7. N. Kirk, *The Growth of Working Class Reformism in Mid-Victorian England* (London, 1984) p. ix.
8. Crossick, *Artisan Elite*, pp. 174-98; idem, 'Social Structure and Working-class Behaviour: Kentish London, 1840-1880', London Ph.D. thesis 1976; see also R.Q. Gray, *The Labour Aristocracy in Victorian Edinburgh* (Oxford, 1976) pp. 121-7.
9. Crossick, *Artisan Elite*, pp. 181, 196-7.
10. T.R. Tholfsen, *Working-class Radicalism in Mid-Victorian England* (London, 1976) pp. 292-3.
11. Kirk, *The Growth of Working Class Reformism*, pp. 220-1.
12. A. Howkins, *Whitsun in 19th Century Oxfordshire* (Oxford, 1973);

Notes for pages 4-5

idem, 'The Taming of Whitsun: the changing face of a nineteenth-century rural holiday', in E. and S. Yeo (eds), *Popular Culture and Class Conflict 1590-1914* (Brighton, 1981) pp. 187-207. Bob Bushaway also writes of the transformation of Whitsuntide celebrations and the passive support of the gentry of the club day. B. Bushaway, *By Rite: custom, ceremony and community in England 1700-1880* (London, 1982) pp. 260-4.

13. M. Fuller, *West Country Friendly Societies* (Reading, 1964).
14. P. Horn, *Labouring Life in the Victorian Countryside* (Dublin, 1976) p. 150.
15. G.E. Mingay (ed.), *The Victorian Countryside*, vol. 2 (London, 1981) p. 581. The affiliated orders are given two sentences.
16. A. Howkins, *Poor Labouring Men: rural radicalism in Norfolk 1870-1923* (London, 1985).
17. B.B. Gilbert, *The Evolution of National Insurance in Great Britain* (London, 1966); P. Thane, *The Foundations of the Welfare State* (London, 1982); B.B. Gilbert, 'The Decay of Nineteenth-century Provident Institutions and the coming of Old Age Pensions in Great Britain', *Economic History Review*, 17, 1964-5, 551-63; S. Yeo, 'Working-class Association, Private Capital, Welfare and the State in the Late-nineteenth and Twentieth Centuries' in N. Parry, M. Rustin and C. Satyamurti (eds), *Social Work, Welfare and the State* (London, 1979) pp. 48-71; P. Thane, 'Non-contributory versus Insurance Pensions 1878-1908' in P. Thane, ed., *The Origins of British Social Policy* (London, 1978) pp. 84-106; J.H. Treble, 'The Attitudes of Friendly Societies towards the Movement in Great Britain for State Pensions 1878-1908', *International Review of Social History*, 15, 1970, 266-99; C.G. Hanson, 'Welfare before the Welfare State', in R.M. Hartwell and others (eds), *The Long Debate on Poverty* (London, 1972) pp. 113-39.
18. D.G. Green, *Working Class Patients and the Medical Establishment* (London, 1985); P. Johnson, *Saving and Spending: the working-class economy in Britain 1870-1939* (Oxford, 1985); idem, p. 127 'Credit and Thrift and the British Working Class, 1870-1939', in J. Winter (ed.), *The Working Class in Modern British History* (Cambridge, 1983) pp. 147-70;

Notes for pages 5-8

H. Marland, *Medicine and Society in Wakefield and Huddersfield 1780-1870* (Cambridge, 1987).

19. Marland p. 184; Johnson, *Saving and Spending*, p. 57; Green, *Working Class Patients*, p. 96.
20. Wilkinson, *Mutual Thrift*, p. 189. Wilkinson claims that the returns made to the Chief Registrar were 'worse than useless, misleading lights along a not too easy path; a waste of public money'.
21. Gosden, *Friendly Societies*, p. 245; Hobsbawm, 'Friendly Societies', p. 98. In the excellent catalogue of Scottish labour records the information on friendly societies is largely confined to listing printed and manuscript rule books, I. MacDougall, *A Catalogue of Some Labour Records in Scotland*, Scottish Labour History Society (Edinburgh, 1978) pp. 1-42. The authors of the detailed studies of friendly societies in the West Country and Kentish London each only used one manuscript minute book of a local society or branch. Fuller, *West Country Friendly Societies* p. 164; Crossick, *Artisan Elite*, pp. 285-7.
22. Hobsbawm, 'Friendly Societies', p. 99; D. Neave, 'The Local Records of Affiliated Friendly Societies', *Local Historian*, 16, 1984, 161-9; idem, 'Victorian Self-help and the Local Community', *Local History*, 1, July 1984, 10-11.
23. For details see Neave, thesis, pp. 421-5.
24. Johnson, *Saving and Spending*, p. 60.
25. Recent local studies include: Rex C. Russell, *Friendly Societies in the Caistor, Binbrook and Brigg Area in the Nineteenth Century* (Nettleton, 1975); J.J. Turner, 'The Growth and Development of Friendly Societies in Cleveland and Teesside *c*.1835-1914: a preliminary research note', *Cleveland and Teesside Local History Bulletin*, 48, 1985, 22-36; R.P. Hastings, *Essays in North Riding History 1780-1850* (Northallerton, 1981) Chapter VII pp. 110-23 'Self-help'; Dot Jones, 'Did Friendly Societies Matter?: a study of friendly society membership in Glamorgan 1794-1910', *Welsh History Review*, 12, 1985, 324-49; J. O'Neill 'Self-Help in Nottinghamshire: The Woodborough Male Friendly Society, 1826-1954', *Transactions of the Thoroton Society*, 90, 1986, 57-63; idem, 'A

Notes for pages 8-11

Search for Independence?: Friendly Societies in Nottinghamshire 1724-1912', *Bulletin of Local History East Midland Region*, 13, 1988, 11-15; G. Hothersall, 'Friendly Societies in West Sussex 1794-1875', *West Sussex History*, no. 35, Sept. 1986, 18-22, no. 36, Jan. 1987, 12-18; no. 37, May 1987 25-30; D. Neave, *Feasts, Fellowship and Financial Aid: South Holderness Friendly Societies* (Beverley, 1986); idem, *East Riding Friendly Societies* (East Yorkshire Local History Series, 41, Beverley, 1988).

1. The Rural East Riding: The Victorian Background

1. K.J. Allison, *The East Riding of Yorkshire Landscape* (London, 1976) pp. 221-53; idem, (ed.), *Victoria History of the County of York, East Riding* (VCH ER) vol. 1 (London, 1969) p. 215.
2. K.A. MacMahon, *Roads and Turnpike Trusts in Eastern Yorkshire* (York, 1964); idem, *The Beginnings of the East Yorkshire Railways* (York, 1974); B.F. Duckham, *The Inland Waterways of East Yorkshire 1700-1900* (York, 1972).
3. M.G. Adams, 'Agricultural Change in the East Riding of Yorkshire 1850-1880', Ph.D. thesis, Hull, 1977; A. Harris, *The Rural Landscape of the East Riding of Yorkshire 1700-1850* (London, 1961) pp. 97-123.
4. B. English, 'Patterns of Estate Management in East Yorkshire *c*.1840-*c*.1880', *Agricultural History Review*, vol. 32, 1984, p. 29; J.T. Ward, *East Yorkshire Landed Estates in the Nineteenth Century* (York, 1967).
5. Lord Londesborough with 33,000 acres was resident only for a few weeks at the most each year. D. Neave, *Londesborough: history of an East Yorkshire estate village* (Londesborough, 1977) pp. 21-8; Lord Leconfield of Petworth with 13,000 acres had no large house in the county, Ward, *East Yorkshire Landed Estates*, pp. 29-30, 72.
6. Borthwick Institute of Historical Research (BIHR) 1865 Visitation Returns (V/Ret. 1865) Foston, Shipton, Acklam, and Burton Agnes.
7. Ibid., Catwick. Similar classifications occur in other returns; at

Notes for pages 11-12

Brandesburton it was the 'opulent and educated' who attended church, and at Hutton Cranswick the people 'of some standing and education'. The 'labouring poor' were either active Methodists or attended no place of worship 'preferring a day's idleness to a day's spiritual improvement' or, as a more understanding incumbent in an estate village commented they liked 'to show that they are their own master on Sunday'. Ibid., Brandesburton, Hutton Cranswick, Newbald, Atwick and Escrick; the Anglican farmers at Catwick were not typical, many farmers were nonconformists. At Londesborough three of the principal farmers were Independents and at Atwick seven of the eleven farmers were dissenters. Others were said to be indifferent to religion and to the spiritual and moral condition of their servants and children. Farmers were criticised for neglecting to use 'the influence which their position gave them'. The clergy did not identify themselves with the farmers whom they felt were in need of a higher and sounder education than they were receiving. In some cases the farms were in the hands of 'ignorant hinds'. Ibid., Londesborough, Atwick, Burnby, Cherry Burton, Dunnington, Easington, Market Weighton and Burton Agnes.

8. J.D. Gay, *The Geography of Religion in England* (London, 1971) pp. 271, 305, 309; A. Everitt, *The Pattern of Rural Dissent: the nineteenth century* (Leicester, 1972) p. 69; R. Currie, 'A Micro-theory of Methodist Growth', *Proceedings of the Wesley Historical Society*, 36, 1967, 71.
9. For an informative and entertaining contemporary account of Primitive Methodism in the East Riding see H. Woodcock, *Piety amongst the Peasantry* (London, 1889).
10. J.A. Sheppard, 'East Yorkshire's Agricultural Labour Force in the Mid-nineteenth Century', *Agricultural History Review*, ix, 1961, 43-54.
11. J.P. Dunbabin, 'The Incidence and Organization of Agricultural Trades Unionism in the 1870s' *Agricultural History Review*, xvi, 1968, 123-4; see also table in K.D.M. Snell, *Annals of the Labouring Poor: social change and agrarian England 1660-1900* (Cambridge, 1985) pp. 96-7.

Notes for page 12

12. A. Kussmaul, *Servants in Husbandry in Early Modern England* (Cambridge, 1981) pp. 23, 120-1; Dunbabin, 'Incidence', p. 124, Snell, p. 95.
13. J. Eddowes, *Martinmas Musings; or Thoughts about the Hiring-day* (Driffield 1854) pp. 7-8.
14. S. Caunce, 'East Riding Hiring Fairs', *Oral History*, 3, autumn 1975, 45-52; M. Reed 'Social Change and Social Conflict in Nineteenth Century England: a comment', *The Journal of Peasant Studies*, 12, 1984, 111-13. For contemporary criticisms of hirings fairs and living-in in the East Riding see F.O. Morris, *The Present System of Hiring Farm Servants in the East Riding of Yorkshire with Suggestions for its Improvement* (Driffield, 1854); J. Eddowes, *The Agricultural Labourer as he really is; or, Village Morals in 1854* (Driffield, 1854); idem, *Martinmas Musings*; W. Barugh, *Master and Man*, (Driffield, 1854); J. Skinner, *Facts and Opinions concerning Statute Hirings* (London, 1861). There are numerous newspaper accounts of farm servants acquiring enhanced wages, e.g. *HA*, 19/11/1859, 17/11/1860, 22/11/1862. See also 'Report by Mr. Edward Wilkinson upon the Poor Law Union of Driffield', Royal Commission on Labour: The Agricultural Labourer, PP 1893-4, [C. 6894-VI] XXXV p. 62.
15. Dunbabin, 'Incidence and Organization', 120-4.
16. G. Legard, 'Farming in the East Riding of Yorkshire', *Journal of the Royal Agricultural Society*, 9, 1848, 125; In England only the agricultural labourers in Northumberland, Durham, Lancashire, West and North Ridings, and Cumberland and Durham were usually paid more than the East Riding labourer. Figures for all counties in 1867-70, 1898, and 1907 are given in E.H. Hunt, *Regional Wage Variations in Britain 1850-1914* (Oxford, 1973) pp. 61-4.
17. Dunbabin, 'Incidence and Organization', 124 n.2; Hobsbawm and Rudé, *Captain Swing*, Appendix 1; A. Charlesworth, (ed.), *An Atlas of Rural Protest in Britain 1548-1900* (London, 1983).
18. I. Carter, 'Agricultural Workers in the Class Structure: a critical note', *Sociological Review*, 22, 1974, 271-9; H. Newby, *The Deferential Worker* (Harmondsworth, 1977).

Notes for pages 14-15

2. The Arrival and Spread of the Affiliated Orders in the East Riding

1. Neave, thesis, pp. 95-8; Humberside County Record Office (HCRO) QDC/2 and QSV/1; P. Davis, *The Old Friendly Societies of Hull* (Hull, 1926). For full list of societies see Neave, *East Riding Friendly Societies*, pp. 41-71.
2. Hull University Library (HUL) DX/150/26/14; HCRO, DDBC 22/section B. p. 633, DDMT/285, QDC/2; Beverley Library, Beverley broadsides pamphlet 30; *Hull Rockingham* 6/10/1832 reference from E. Gillett.
3. Hobsbawm and Rudé, *Captain Swing*, pp. 49-63, appendix 3 pp. 17-19, 23; W.W. Rostow, *British Economy of the Nineteenth Century* (London, 1948) pp. 111-12; HCRO DDX/216 Robert Sharp's journal 12/7/1827, 14, 19 and 23/1/1830 8/7/1830, 16/11/1830, 5, 14 and 12/12/1830, 7/7/1831, 12/7/1832, 8/2/1833, 11/7/1833, 10/7/1834, 9/7/1835. For Robert Sharp see D. Neave, (ed.), *South Cave: a market village community in the 18th and 19th centuries* (Howden, 2nd ed., 1984) pp. 514; P. Howorth, *Driffield 1700-1860* (Driffield, 1980) p. 56; Diaries of Revd Richard Allen of Driffield, 1828, 1830, 1832, in possession of Mr Gamble, Scarborough, 1974. In the North Riding many men were said to have gone unhired at the hirings each year from 1826 to 1833. At Malton hirings, few farm servants were engaged in 1830 and in 1831-2 strong boys and young women at low wages were still preferred to men. Hastings, *Essays*, pp. 62-3; *YG* 11, 18 and 24/12/1830, 15, 22 and 29/1/1831; 26/2/1831; N.D. Hopkin, 'The Old and New Poor Law in East Yorkshire *c.* 1760-1850', Leeds M. Phil 1968, pp. 26-7.
4. Diary of Revd Richard Allen 22/4/1830.
5. C.D. Hebden, *The Trustee Savings Banks of Yorkshire and Lincoln* (1981) p. 350.
6. For brief account of the origins of the chief affiliated orders see appendix A below.
7. Neave, thesis, pp. 99-101.
8. Ancient Order of Foresters dispensation book, Ancient Order of Foresters national office, Southampton.

Notes for pages 16-19

9. *HA*, 27/7/1838.
10. 'Forestry in Hull and Neighbourhood', *Directory of the AOF 1890*, pp. xlvi; *Foresters Miscellany* 1842, pp. 28-9.
11. Neave, thesis, pp. 530-1.
12. Loyal Order of Ancient Shepherds (LOAS), Ashton Unity, register of Lodges 1826-89, LOAS Head office, Stockport.
13. *YG*, 2/2/1839.
14. Ibid., 20/5/1837, 3/3 and 16/6/1838, 8/6/1839, 6/6/1840; *Hull Advertiser*, 2/3/1838; D.J. Salmon, *Malton in the Early 19th Century* (Northallerton, 1981) p. 55.
15. The 'gorsedd' - the stone circle of the Druids was an eighteenth century invention, S. Piggott, *The Druids* (Harmondsworth, 1974) pp. 142-3; *YG*, 8/6/1839; *HA* 1/11/1839, 14/8/1840; HCRO, DDX/61 records of Harpham Druids 1846-1913.
16. R. Campbell, *Rechabite History* (Manchester, 1911) pp. 47-8, 73, 162.
17. E. Hobsbawm, *Labouring Men* (London, 1968) p. 131.
18. Gosden, *Friendly Societies*, p. 237.
19. *YG*, 6/9 and 4/10/1834 quoted in Hastings, *Essays*, p. 118.
20. First Annual Report of the Poor Law Commissioners, PP 1835, (500), XXXV pp. 55-6; Fourth Annual Report of the Poor Law Commissioners, PP 1837-8, (147), XXVIII, p. 247.
21. *HA*, 29/3/1839.
22. C. Hardwick, *A Manual for Friendly Societies* (London, 1859) p. 32, quoted in Gosden, *Friendly Societies*, p. 198.
23. HCRO PUA 1/1, PUB 1/1, PUD 1/1; PUH 1/1; PUP 1/1-2.
24. Ibid., PUB 1/1. PUD 1/1; J.J. Sheahan and T. Whellan, *History and Topography of the City of York and the East Riding of Yorkshire*, vol. 2 (Beverley, 1856) pp. 340, 392, 452, 563, 604.
25. Neave, thesis, appendix 1; T. Bulmer, *History and Directory of East Yorkshire* (Preston, 1892) pp. 167-8.
26. Third Annual Report of the Poor Law Commissioners, PP 1837, (546), XXXI, pp. 90-1.
27. Public Record Office (PRO) FS 1/796 Yorks 19 Rules of the Etton Amicable and Friendly Society 1837, 1840, 1845; ibid., 1/817 Yorks. 328 Rules of the Etton Female Friendly Society 26, May 1841.

Notes for pages 20-2

28. HCRO, PUD 1/1 Driffield Poor Law Union minute book October 1836; BIHR, Middleton on the Wolds glebe terriers; *Hull Rockingham*, 3/8/1833.
29. *BG*, 22/6/1861; *DT*, 22/6/1861; AOF Middleton proposition and minute books, court records with court secretary at Middleton on the Wolds 1982; AOF Lockington proposition and minute books, court records with court secretary at Lockington 1980; IOOF MU Lund minute book, lodge records in Oddfellows' Hall, Lund, 1980.
30. *Foresters' Miscellany*, 1842, pp. 131-2.
31. *HA*, 17/7/1840, 7/7/1848; *Oddfellows Quarterly Magazine*, viii, Jan 1844-Oct 1845, pp. 208-9.
32. T. Clarke, *History of Howden* (Howden, 1851) p. 61.
33. Hastings, *Essays*, p. 119.
34. *HA*, 18 and 25/2/1842.
35. Ibid., 18/2/1842.

3. Fluctuating Fortunes

1. A certain Christopher Thomson who kept a reading room and library next to the Peoples' College, Orchard Street, Sheffield produced at least two *Tracts for Odd Fellows and Social Reformers* in 1849 which were aimed at reforming and democratising the Nottingham Imperial Order of Oddfellows to which he belonged. He attacked its centralisation and the power of the Grand Lodge: 'Let us look at our own Society, the Nottingham Order of Odd Fellows, it has one of those paper Constitutions which decrees that the Grand Lodge "shall always assemble in Nottingham". That the members possess the "sole right" of making and altering all laws by which the society is to be governed; it is likewise the high court of appeal in disputed cases - can make lodges of degrees, and confer rewards of crimson rosettes, and silver stars, and pocket salaries, and do many other things which all men, who are responsible to themselves alone can do'. *Tracts for Odd Fellows and Social Reformers*, no. 2, May 1849, p. 18.
2. T.B. Stead, *A Short History of the Chief Affiliated Friendly Societies*

Notes for pages 22-7

(Leeds, 1880) pp. 40-1; C. Walford, *Insurance Cyclopaedia*, vol. iv (London, 1878) pp. 400-1.

3. Ibid. Walford, p. 401.
4. E. Crew, *Loyal Order of Ancient Shepherds Centenary Souvenir* (Manchester, 1926) pp. 41-5.
5. Loyal Order of Ancient Shepherds, *Annual Meeting Reports* 1849-56.
6. T.B. Stead, 'Historical Sketch of the Order', *Directory of the Ancient Order of Foresters 1896* (Dundee, 1896) pp. xxi-ii.
7. R. Highet, *Rechabite History* (Manchester, 1936) p. 501.
8. Ibid., pp. 62-3, 67-8.
9. Ibid., pp. 93-4.
10. Ibid., pp. 96-97, 501.
11. Stead, *Short History*, p. 41.
12. Neave, *East Riding Friendly Societies*, pp. 41-71.
13. *HA*, 23/6, 21/7/1848.
14. Neave, *East Riding Friendly Societies*, pp. 48-9, 54, 71.
15. HCRO, DDX 17/15; M.W. Barley (ed.), *History of Driffield* (Hull, 1938); F. Ross, *Contributions towards a History of Driffield* (Driffield, 1898); Howorth, *Driffield*; D. Neave, *Driffield: a town trail* (Beverley, 1981).
16. Numbers of public houses calculated from trade directories 1830-51.
17. Neave, thesis, pp. 478-9. Evidence suggests that there may have been three early local societies. The parish note book of the Revd Joseph Carter of Bainton, *c.* 1834, records parishioners being members of Driffield Union Society and Driffield Old Club. HCRO PR/898. The diaries of Revd Richard Allen, vicar of Driffield, 1828, 1830, and 1832 refer to the feast days of the Union Society and the New Club.
18. Neave, thesis, pp. 479-80.
19. *HA*, 24/5/1850.
20. Ibid., 14/6/1850.
21. *Ancient Order of Foresters' Court Directory*, 1845-52. Court Olive Branch founded in 1842 had only six members when it was closed in 1850. During its eight year existence it never had more than nine members.

Notes for pages 27-32

22. HCRO, DDX 61/1 Harpham District Druids account and minute book 1846-64.
23. *HA*, 12/7/1850.
24. Ibid., 18/7/1851.
25. Ibid., 29/7/1854.
26. Ibid., 17/7/1840, 12/7/1850; *DT*, 15/7/1865.
27. *HA*, 18/7/1845; *YG*, 19/7/1845.
28. *HA*, 19/7/1862.
29. Ross, *Contributions*, p. 91; Davis, *The Old Friendly Societies*, p. 8.
30. *HA*, 22/2/1849, 27/1/1854, 12/5/55; *ECH*, 9/3 and 22/6/1848; *YG*, 20/1/1849; Yorkshire Union of Mechanics' Institutes, *Annual Reports*, 1850, 1852, 1853.
31. HCRO, MRB, MRP, MRQ.
32. R. Currie, *Methodism Divided* (London, 1968) p. 95.
33. Primitive Methodist Connexion, *Minutary Records*, 1845-55.
34. HCRO, MRQ, MRD.
35. Chapel building dates from Sheahan and Whellan, *History and Topography*, T. Bulmer, *History and Directory of East Yorkshire*, and Religious Census Returns 1851.
36. H.O. Horne, *A History of Savings Banks* (London, 1947) pp. 118-36; Gosden, *Self-Help*, pp. 221-4.
37. Hebden, *Trustee Savings Bank*, pp. 128-30; *HA*, 7/12/1849, 1, 8/2, 24/5/1850.
38. Gosden, *Self-Help*, p. 222 n. 2.
39. Hebden, *Trustee Savings Bank*, p. 170.
40. AOF Middleton minute and proposition book 1, 24/5/1850. In 1853 5791 friendly societies had deposits in savings banks, *Driffield Observer*, 21/12/1853. In 1850 ten societies had money in the Bridlington Savings Bank, *HA*, 8/2/1850.
41. HCRO, PUH 3/1 Howden Union Letter Book.
42. A.D. Gayer, W.W. Rostow, and A.J. Schwartz, *The Growth and Fluctuation of the British Economy 1790-1850* vol.1 (Oxford, 1953) pp. 276-7, 306-7; T. Tooke and W. Newmarch, *A History of Prices* vol. v. (London, 1928) pp. 8-9, 12-13, 16-17, 21, 27, 34-5.
43. *HA*, 28/12/1849.

Notes for pages 34-7

44. Neave, thesis, p. 149 Table 20.
45. IOOF MU Lund minute and contribution books.
46. HCRO, DDBD 87/126; A.L. Bowley, 'The Statistics of Wages in the United Kingdom during the Last Hundred Years: Pt. 1. Agricultural wages', *Journal of the Royal Statistical Society*, 61, 702-22; idem, 62, 565-70; A Wilson Fox, 'Agricultural Wages in England and Wales during the Last Half Century', JRSS 66, 273-348; 'Report by Mr. Wilson Fox on the Wages and Earnings of Agricultural Labourers in the United Kingdom', PP 1900 [C.346] LXXXII, 557; 'Second Report by Mr. Wilson Fox . . . ', PP 1905 XCVII, 335; C.S. Orwin and B.I. Felton, 'A Century of Wages and Earnings in Agriculture', *Journal of the Royal Agricultural Society*, 92, 1931, 231-57.
47. *HA*, 9/11/1849.
48. Ibid., 16/11/1849.
49. Ibid., 16, 23, 30/11, 7/12/1849; *Hull Packet*, 30/11/1849. In January 1850 there were reports from the area around York of a 'great scarcity of work' on the land and wage decreases of 25% and one-sixth. Armstrong, *Stability and Change*, p. 106.
50. *HA*, 4/1, 15/2/1850.
51. Ibid., 11/1, 31/5/1850.
52. 33rd general report of the Emigration Commissioners, PP 1873, [C. 768] XVIII, appendix 1.
53. *HA*, 9/11/1849, 12/4, 3, 10, 24/5, 21/6, 5, 19/7, 2, 9, 16, 23/8/1850, 2/5/1851.
54. Ibid., 12/4/1850.
55. Howorth, *Driffield*, pp. 86, 88.
56. *Driffield Observer*, 21/12/1853.
57. E.L. Jones, *Seasons and Prices* (London, 1964) pp. 169-75.
58. Adams, thesis, pp. 145, 353.
59. HCRO, uncalendared AOF Keyingham contribution books.
60. Neave, thesis, pp. 529-35.
61. A.B. Erickson, 'The Cattle Plague in England 1865-67', *Agricultural History*, 35, 1961, 94-103; Adams, thesis, p. 36.
62. *ECH*, 13/8, 18/10, 4/11, 18/11/1865; 13, 20, 27/1/1866.
63. IOOF MU Lund contribution books 1839-69 and minute books 1839-80.

Notes for pages 37-41

64. HCRO AOF Keyingham contribution book.
65. AOF Middleton minute and proposition book 1839-91 and contribution book 2.
66. *DT,* 2/2/1872.
67. Neave, thesis, p. 142 Fig. 11.
68. HCRO, AOF Keyingham contribution book.
69. HCRO, MRD uncalendared.
70. R.C. Russell, *The 'Revolt of the Field' in Lincolnshire* (Barton on Humber, 1956) pp. 39-40; Adams, thesis, pp. 362-7; *ECH,* 27/2, 29/2, 7/3, 11/4/1872; *BG,* 10/2/1872; *DT,* 28/12/1872.
71. Adams, thesis, p. 361.
72. There is nothing to indicate whether the campaign launched by the Local Government Board in the early 1870s against outdoor relief resulted in any increase in friendly society recruitment paralleling the situation in the late 1830s when the New Poor Law was first implemented, but this is possible, M.E. Rose, *The Relief of Poverty 1834-1914* (London, 1972) p. 21.
73. Gilbert, 'The Decay of Nineteenth-century Provident Institutions', 552-63.
74. Neave, thesis, appendix 1 for individual societies.
75. Report of the Chief Registrar of Friendly Societies 1880, PP 1881 (414) LXXXIV; ibid 1887, PP 1889 (113) LXXI.
76. PRO, FS 3/422 Yorks 22.
77. Report by Mr R. Hunter Pringle on South Durham and selected districts of the North and East Ridings of Yorkshire, Royal Commission on Agriculture, PP 1895, [C. 7735] XVI, pp. 8-10.
78. Adams, thesis, p. 362.
79. AOF Middleton, proposition and minute book 1839-91.
80. IOOF MU Hutton Cranswick, contribution books 1861-82, 1883-1910. Lodge records with lodge secretary, Driffield, 1980.
81. AOF Lockington, proposition and minute book 1840-85.
82. Population returns 1801-1901 in W. Page, (ed.), *Victoria County History of Yorkshire*, vol. 2, (London, 1912) pp. 487-99.
83. Hunt, *Regional Wage*, pp. 17, 36, 63.
84. Royal Commission on the Aged Poor, PP 1895 [C. 7684-1], XIV, pp. 354, 368.
85. There were juvenile Foresters branches opened at Beverley in

Notes for pages 41-44

1877, Welton and Hessle 1886, Sutton-on-Hull 1887, and Bridlington 1888 and juvenile Oddfellows at Elloughton 1888 and at Beverley, Bishop Burton, Hutton Cranswick, Lund and Long Riston by the end of the century. AOF *Directory*, 1896, pp. 449-51; IOOF MU *Directory and List of Lodges*, 1940, pp. 32, 165. The AOF took the lead in the establishment of juvenile branches. Wilkinson, *Mutual Thrift*, p. 181.

86. AOF Hutton Cranswick proposition book 1868-1943. Court records at Foresters' Hall, Hutton Cranswick, 1980.
87. Neave, thesis, p. 183.
88. A. Wilson and H. Levy, *Industrial Assurance* (London, 1937) pp. 36-8.
89. Report of Edward Wilkinson upon the Poor Law Union of Driffield, Royal Commission on Labour: The Agricultural Labourer, PP 1893-4 [C. 6894] XXXV, p. 62.
90. *Parish Magazine Union,* July 1908 p. 199.
91. Ibid., pp. 200-1.
92. Ibid., Gosden, *Self-Help,* pp. 106-7.
93. *Parish Magazine Union,* Sept. 1908 p. 253.
94. Ibid. Sept. 1912 pp. 210-12.
95. Treble, 'The Attitudes of Friendly Societies', 266-99; Gilbert, 'The Decay of Nineteenth-century Provident Institutions', 552-63; idem *The Evolution of National Insurance*, pp. 159-232, 289-447; Neave, thesis, pp. 400-3.
96. ibid., p. 186.
97. HCRO AOF Keyingham contribution book.
98. IOOF MU Lund minute and contribution book.
99. At least twenty-eight societies still existed in 1980: IOOF MU branches at Beverley (2 lodges), Bishop Burton, Elloughton, North Ferriby, Hutton Cranswick, Lund and Long Riston; AOF branches at Beverley, Bishop Wilton, Bridlington, Driffield, Hutton Cranswick, Keyingham, Lockington, Middleton, and Sutton-on-Hull; GUOOF branches at Norton, Etton and Leconfield (united); UAOD branches at Beverley, Leven and Preston; NUOFG branches at Beverley and Cottingham; LOAS branch at Nafferton; the independent Loyal Oddfellows Good Samaritan Society at Hedon and the female friendly society at

Notes for pages 44-51

Holme upon Spalding Moor.

4. The Club and the Village Community

1. For Keyingham Foresters see Neave, *Feasts, Fellowship and Financial Aid*, pp. 9-12.
2. Neave, thesis, p. 274 Table 66.
3. AOF Lockington proposition and minute books 1840-1912, register book 1912.
4. IOOF MU Lund contribution books and sickness registers.
5. Everitt, *Pattern of Rural Dissent*, p. 44.
6. Hobsbawm and Rudé, *Captain Swing*, p. 158.
7. Neave, thesis pp. 253-6.
8. Royal Commission on Agriculture, PP 1881, [C. 2778-11] XVI, pp. 159-60; D. Neave, 'The Wenlocks and Wheldrake' in D.R. Brown (ed.), *Wheldrake Aspects of a Yorkshire Village* (Wheldrake, 1971) pp. 20-3; PRO FS 3/141.
9. *DT*, 19/7/1862.
10. Sheahan and Whellan, vol. 2, p. 485.
11. Census enumerators' returns 1861, microfilm, Beverley Library.
12. F.O. Morris, *Possibilities in a Parish* (London, 1850) p. 3; Allison (ed.) *VCH ER* vol. 2 (London, 1974) p. 295. There was a flourishing Wesleyan day school in the village from 1847-1912, an unusual feature in the East Riding, ibid., Allison p. 296.
13. BIHR Bp. V/Ret. 1868 visitation returns.
14. Morris, *Possibilities*, p. 9.
15. *Poll Book: East Riding Election 1868* (Beverley, 1868).
16. *DT*, 5/8/1865; HCRO MRD 1/1 Driffield Wesleyan Circuit baptism register 1837-67.
17. Census enumerators' returns 1861.
18. *DT*, 13/7/1861.
19. W. White, *History, Gazetteer, and Directory of the East and North Ridings of Yorkshire* (Sheffield, 1840).
20. A report of the opening of a lodge at Barton-on-Humber by the Hull and Beverley district of the LOAS contains the following account of such unofficial missionary work: 'The above lodge had previously been opened with the title of "United Shepherd"

Notes for pages 51-8

by a party of men who have for some time been going round the country, stating themselves to be Shepherds, but in fact, do not belong to the order. The members of the above named lodge not being satisfied with the proceedings of these men, applied to the Hull and Beverley district. An application was made to the head of the order and a surance granted. Officers were immediately appointed to open the lodge, which took place as before stated, at the same time the surance from the pretended shepherds was requested by the newly initiated brothers to be brought forward and burnt in the presence of the district officers and brethren of the Faithful Abraham lodge, which request was immediately complied with, to the satisfaction of the parties present. Two other applications have likewise been made from lodges deluded by the same party.' *HA*, 27/12/1839.

21. AOF, *2nd address of the 6th Executive Council*, November 1839.
22. Crew, *Loyal Order of Ancient Shepherds Centenary Souvenir*, p. 31.
23. C. Hardwick, *The History, Present Position, and Social Influence of Friendly Societies* 3rd ed. (London, 1893) p. 150.
24. E.J. Hobsbawm and J.W. Scott, 'Political Shoemakers', *Past and Present*, 89, 1980, 104.
25. Woodcock, *Piety*, p. 71; In South Lindsey craftsmen and shopkeepers provided 49 per cent of Wesleyan local preachers in 1861 and 32 per cent of Primitive Methodist local preachers. Of the Wesleyan local preachers thirteen were grocers and ten shoemakers, the latter were also active as stewards and class leaders. J. Obelkevich, *Religion and Rural Society: South Lindsey 1825-75* (Oxford, 1976) pp. 195-6, 239.
26. Minute books of AOF Middleton, Hutton Cranswick and Keyingham, IOOF MU Hutton Cranswick. HCRO DDX/242 Hunmanby Shepherds minute book.
27. IOOF MU Lund minute book; HCRO DDX/61 Records of Harpham Druids; School log books of Hutton Cranswick and Holme on Spalding Moor at respective schools.
28. Neave, thesis, pp. 230-1.
29. Allison (ed.), *VCH ER* vol. v (Oxford, 1984) p. 55.
30. HCRO QDE/1 Land tax returns Keyingham 1832.

Notes for pages 58-60

31. Allison (ed.) *VCH ER* vol. v, pp. 55-9; HCRO QDE/1.
32. Census enumerators' returns 1851.
33. Allison (ed.) *VCH ER*, vol. v, pp. 57, 64.
34. Religious census returns 1851, microfilm HCRO; BIHR Bp. V. 1894/Ret., 1894 visitation returns Keyingham.
35. HCRO AOF Keyingham contribution and cash books; Neave, *Feasts, Fellowship and Financial Aid*, pp. 9-12.
36. AOF *Directory* 1845, 1860, 1870, 1879.
37. AOF *Directory* 1868, 1896.
38. HCRO DDPK 18/5 List of Keyingham Foresters' Trustees 1876-1910.
39. Religious census returns 1851 Burstwick.
40. AOF Keyingham cash book.
41. Ibid. contribution books; HCRO MRW Baptism books of Patrington Branch Primitive Methodist Connexion 1843-74; Patrington Primitive Methodist Circuit Plans; Monumental inscriptions in Methodist Church, Keyingham, 1980.
42. Census enumerators' returns 1871; AOF Keyingham membership book; HCRO SBM Keyingham School Board minutes 1873-1903; ibid., DDPK/18/5.
43. HCRO SBM Keyingham School Board minutes 1873-1903.
44. Census enumerators' returns 1871; AOF Keyingham membership book; Monumental inscription Keyingham Methodist Church; HCRO SBM Keyingham School Board minutes 1873-1903; ibid. DDPK/18/5; ibid. PR/3287 Vestry minute book; information from M.H. Smith, Keyingham.
45. IOOF MU *List of Lodges* 1845-1900.
46. HCRO SBM Keyingham school board minutes 1876.
47. Abstract of quinquennial returns of sickness and mortality from Report of the Chief Registrar of Friendly Societies 1878, App. Pt. II, PP 1880 (109) LXVIII.
48. *HN*, 7/3/1900.
49. Sheahan and Whellan, vol. 2, p. 505.
50. HCRO QDE/1 Land tax returns Hutton Cranswick, 1830.
51. Sheahan and Whellan, vol. 2, p. 505.
52. H. Johnson, *A Tale of Two Villages* (Hutton, 1980) p. 52.
53. HCRO QDE/1.

Notes for pages 60-3

54. Census enumerators' returns 1851.
55. White, *Directory of East Riding*, 1840.
56. Religious census returns 1851.
57. BIHR Bp. V/Ret. 1865 Visitation returns.
58. HCRO SBM Hutton Cranswick, 1872-1902; ibid. Acc 1036 Driffield Primitive Methodist Circuit records; AOF Hutton Cranswick minute books; IOOF MU Hutton Cranswick minute books.
59. *HN*, 17/7/1909; HCRO MRD Driffield Primitive Methodist Circuit Records; AOF Hutton Cranswick minute and proposition book.
60. Census enumerators' returns, Lund 1871; IOOF MU Lund minute book; IOOF MU Hutton Cranswick minute book; HCRO Acc 1036 Driffield Primitive Methodist Circuit Plan 1868; ibid., SBM Hutton Cranswick School Board minute book; South Humberside Area Record Office, Oral History recordings 292/55 George and Ethel Dawson (Ethel Duke) recorded by W.D. Rawson 1973; at the first parish council election for Hutton Cranswick Duke headed the poll by a large margin, *BG*, 22/12/1894.
61. *HA*, 22/2/1839; AOF *Directory of Courts* 1846, 1852, 1860, 1865, 1870, 1880, 1890, 1910.
62. IOOF MU *Quarterly Report*, 1st quarter 1861; IOOF MU *List of Lodges*, 1900, 1913; IOOF MU Hutton Cranswick minute book 1877-1912.
63. LOAS Register of Lodges.
64. AOF Hutton Cranswick proposition books; IOOF MU Hutton Cranswick proposition book 1861-88.
65. Ibid.
66. AOF Hutton Cranswick proposition and minute books.
67. *Hull and East Yorkshire Times* 28/1/1977; Date on Foresters' Hall, Cranswick.
68. Hutton Cranswick School, School Log Book.
69. IOOF MU Hutton Cranswick minute book 25/4/1903; 23/4/1904; AOF Hutton Cranswick minute book 23/5/1896; 7/5/1898; 19/5/1906.
70. Sheahan and Whellan, vol. 2, p. 512; Bulmer, p. 237.

Notes for pages 63-6

71. HCRO QDE/1 Land tax returns Lund 1830.
72. Sheahan and Whellan, vol. 2, p. 512; HCRO DDX/31/558.
73. Census enumerators' returns, 1851.
74. BIHR Bp. V. 1894/Ret. 1894 visitation returns Hutton Cranswick.
75. Religious census returns 1851.
76. Sheahan and Whellan, vol. 2, p. 513.
77. HCRO Acc 1036 Driffield Methodist Circuit Records, Primitive Methodist chapel schedules and circuit plans.
78. Woodcock, *Piety*, p. 113.
79. IOOF MU Lund minute Book 1839-59; inscription to John Robinson in churchyard, Lund.
80. IOOF MU *List of Lodges* 1845; *BG*, 1856-1910 anniversary reports; IOOF MU Lund lodge records.
81. ibid.
82. IOOF MU Lund account book 14 Aug. 1924 and minute book 10 Jan. 1925.
83. *BG*, 14/6/1879, 5/6/1880, 4/6/1881, 3/6/1882.
84. Census enumerators' returns 1851; HCRO PE Lund parish registers; IOOF MU Lund minute book; the lodge made a presentation to him for his 40 years service in March 1894.
85. Woodcock, *Piety*, p. 121.
86. *BG* 22/12/1894, Petch came fifth in the poll out of eleven elected; MI Middleton cemetery; mounted photograph of Wm. Petch in Oddfellows' Hall, Lund, 1980.

5. Membership and Benefits

1. G. Best, *Mid-Victorian Britain 1851-75* (London, 1971) p. 269; Howkins, *Whitsun*, p. 66; Hobsbawm, 'Friendly Societies', 99; Hobsbawm and Rudé, *Captain Swing*, p. 255; Tholfsen states that they 'catered to the upper strata of the working-class', Tholfsen, *Working-class Radicalism*, p. 288.
2. Gilbert, 'The Decay of Nineteenth-century Provident Institutions', 552.
3. Gosden, *Friendly Societies*, pp. 71-88.
4. Quoted in Johnson, *Saving and Spending*, p. 58.

Notes for pages 67-73

5. Quoted in Johnson, 'Credit and Thrift', 183.
6. Gray, *The Labour Aristocracy*, p. 122.
7. Neville Kirk states that the members of Stockport Oddfellows were mainly of craft, skilled and lower-middle class occupations but he rightly comments that it would be wrong to conclude that the affiliated orders were essentially 'aristocratic' in composition. 'Rather their appeal was to the broad mass of regularly employed and relatively well-paid operatives'. Kirk, *The Growth of Working-class Reformism*, pp. 198-9.
8. Crossick, *An Artisan Elite*, pp. 181-3, 189-91.
9. Ibid., p. 181.
10. Royal Commission on the Aged Poor PP 1895, p. 640.
11. P. Mathias, *The First Industrial Nation*, 3rd edn (London, 1983) p. 191. The low and irregular nature of the income of agricultural labourers is the oft quoted reason why they were unlikely to become members of the affiliated orders. e.g. Hobsbawm, 'Friendly Societies' p. 99; Kirk, *The Growth of Working-class Reformism*, p. 198.
12. AOF Middleton proposition book.
13. Gosden, *Friendly Societies*, p. 80.
14. Ibid; Royal Commission on Labour: the agricultural labourer, PP 1893-4 p. 108.
15. AOF Middleton proposition book.
16. Hunt, *Regional Wage*, pp. 85, 105.
17. B.S. Rowntree and M. Kendall, *How the Labourer Lives* (London, 1913) pp. 53-5, 217-25.
18. Royal Commission on the Aged Poor PP 1895, p. 367.
19. Green, *Working-class Patients*, p. 98.
20. Rule books: IOOF MU Beverley 1852, Hessle 1852, Lund 1858, Bp. Burton 1860; AOF Beverley 1859, Pocklington 1851; NUOFG Beverley 1870; UAOD Beverley 1865; LOAS Fulford 1862; GUOOF Cottingham 1864; IOOF KU Beverley 1860: for location see Neave, thesis, pp. 428-34.
21. *Rules of Hutton Cranswick Foresters' Friendly Society* (Driffield, 1899); *Rules of Court Hotham, Ancient Order of Foresters' Friendly Society, Hutton Cranswick* (Driffield, 1906); *Rules of the Keyingham Friendly Society* (Hull, 1905); *Rules of*

Notes for pages 73-9

Court Friendship, Ancient Order of Foresters' Friendly Society, Keyingham (Hull, 1875, 1918); *Rules of Court Foresters' Mount, Ancient Order of Foresters' Friendly Society, Hessle* (Hull, 1880); *Rules of the Loyal St Peter's Lodge, IOOF MU Friendly Society* [Lund] (Beverley, 1880); and *Rules of the Loyal St. Paul's Lodge, IOOF MU Friendly Society*, [Hutton Cranswick] (Driffield, 1884).

22. *Rules of the Loyal Farmers' Refuge Lodge, IOOF MU, Long Riston* (Beverley, 1860).
23. *Rules of Court Beverley, AOF, Beverley* (Beverley, 1859).
24. M.T. Craven, *A New and Complete History of the Borough of Hedon* (Hull, 1972) pp. 200-1. During the summer and autumn of 1849, 1834 people died of cholera in Hull. The town had the highest death rate in the country. Allison, *VCH ER* vol. 1 (London, 1969) p. 234. This epidemic was a severe drain on urban friendly society funds and the Hull district of the Independent Order of Oddfellows, Kingston Unity, suffered particularly and it had to make nine special levies in addition to quarterly ones of a penny per member. As a result Brunswick Lodge, Beverley had its funds reduced to £10 so it chose to leave Hull District and form a district on its own, *National Conference of Friendly Societies Souvenir Handbook* (Hull, 1915) n.p.; *BG*, 3/8/95.
25. Report of the Commissioners on the Poor Law; Appendix B. 1 Pt II, PP 1834, XXXI, pp. 592 a-b, 593 a-b, 594 a-b.; Legard, 'Farming in the East Riding', p. 125; J. Caird, *English Farming in 1850-51* 2nd edn (London, 1968) p. 318.
26. Hopkin, thesis, p. 85. At Pocklington in 1834 the allowance was 3*s* 6*d* per week for an able-bodied man altogether upon the parish, 2*s* 6*d* for his wife, and 10*d* for each child, ibid. p. 57.
27. Royal Commission on Labour: The Agricultural Labourer, PP 1893-4, p. 55.
28. Rowntree and Kendall pp. 116-20, 183-96, 217-26.
29. *Rules of the Loyal Triumph Lodge, Beverley, IOOF MU* (Beverley, 1911) p. 25.
30. Treble, 'The Attitudes of Friendly Societies' pp. 284, 290; in 1903 William Rouse, aged 69, of Souldern, Oxfordshire, received

Notes for pages 79-80

4*s* 6*d* per week from his friendly society. But at the beginning of January 1904, this latter was stopped by the society, 'according to rule for 1 year', and so poor relief of 5*s* 6*d* per week was allowed to Rouse and his wife by the Bicester Board of Guardians during the interim period. P.L.R. Horn, 'Old Age and the Oxfordshire Agricultural Labourer 1870-1914', *Oxoniensa,* 38, 1973, 373-4.

31. HCRO DDX 254/17 *Rules of the Beverley and East Riding District of the National United Order of Free Gardeners Friendly Society* n.d. *c.* 1870. On the subject of exercise the Newbald Benefit Society had the following comment: 'As exercise is allowed to be conducive to health, by putting the different organs of the body in proper action, they will be allowed to walk about, providing they do not take too violent exercise, such as running, leaping, or the like, but take all necessary measures for the recovery of their health, which we trust every Member of this Society will observe and do.' *Rules of Newbald Benefit Society* (Beverley, 1850) p. 9.
32. *Rules of the Loyal Farmers' Refuge Lodge, Long Riston, IOOF MU* (Beverley, 1860) p. 14; in 1863 Henry Thurlow brought a charge, to Middleton Foresters' court, against Thomas Thurlow for working while receiving sick benefit. AOF Middleton minute book 7 January 1863.
33. IOOF MU Lund minute book July-October 1846.
34. HCRO uncalendared IOOF MU Elloughton District minute book 27 June 1868.
35. IOOF MU Long Riston minute book 28 March and 25 April 1868.
36. AOF Lockington minute book 2, 4/10/1886, 28/11/1887, 31/12/1889, 29/6/1891, 11/5/1892, 26/10/1894.
37. IOOF MU Lund minute books. Wood's son and successor who was the lodge surgeon in the 1860s was also charged with neglect and non-attendance in 1868 but at the next meeting was re-elected to his post.

    Some branches made additional arrangements concerning medical treatment for their members. In December 1848 Hutton Cranswick Foresters voted thirty-six to four in favour of

Notes for pages 80-1

a proposal to purchase for ten guineas 'Mr Halse's Galvanic Apparatus' for the use of Foresters and their wives. When the galvanising machine arrived in February 1849 it was put in the care of two members John Hodgson and William Denton who were to receive fourteen shillings a week between them 'for their labours for the next month'. The following month it passed to two other members and then in April to George Spink who undertook to pay one guinea for the use of it and to 'keep her in good repair and any of the Foresters have ackses to it for paying sixpence each time for twelve months to April 21 1850'. Spink retained it the following year for ten shillings. The initial enthusiasm for the machine soon passed and for four years it is not mentioned in the minute book until in 1854 it was proposed that it be sold on the feast day to the highest bidder. The machine however was not sold and the final reference to it is in July 1855 when it was proposed and seconded 'that John Hodgson bring forward the Galvanic Appratus [*sic*] to give us a satisfactory answer where the Galvanic Appratus [*sic*] is or be suspended until he comply before this day Month', AOF Hutton Cranswick minute books.

38. IOOF MU Long Riston minute book, records with lodge secretary Long Riston 1978.
39. D.G. Green, 'Doctors versus Workers', *Economic Affairs*, vol. 5, no. 1, Oct.-Dec. 1984, supplement p. iv.
40. Ibid., iv-vi; Ruth G. Hodgkinson, *The Origins of the National Health Service* (London, 1967) pp. 602-10; R.W. Harris, *National Health Insurance in Great Britain 1911-46* (London, 1946) pp. 147-52; Gosden, *Friendly Societies*, pp. 147-8.
41. For the travelling system and allowances of trade unions see Hobsbawm's essay on 'The Tramping Artisan' in E.J. Hobsbawm, *Labouring Men* (London, 1968) pp. 34-63, and R.A. Leeson, *Travelling Brothers* (St Albans, 1979).
42. *Rules of the Loyal St Peter's Lodge , IOOF MU* (Beverley, 1858) p. 3; *Laws for the Government and Guidance of the Friendly Society called the Grand United Order of Odd-Fellows* (Leeds, 1865) p.1.
43. Ibid., pp. 28-32.; J. Thornley, *History of the Grand United Order*

Notes for pages 81-3

of Oddfellows 3 vols (Manchester, 1911-13) pt 3, pp. 40-51.

44. Gosden, *Friendly Societies*, pp. 76-7, 221. The AOF travelling allowance was 1*s* 3*d* per day; HCRO DDX 254/21 *Rules of the National United Order of Free Gardeners 1878* (Oldham, 1879) p. 40. Travelling 'diplomas' not to be granted in case of a turn-out, cf. similar IOOF MU rule re strikes Gosden, *Friendly Societies*, p. 221; DDX 61/11 *UAOD Constitutional Rules* (Hull, 1891) p. 50 - travelling relief.
45. Only one reference was found in a search through ten rural branch minute books. IOOF MU Lund minute book 2, 6 Oct. 1865 Past Grand Cass granted travelling card which he returned 4 Nov. In May 1841 Hutton Cranswick AOF paid 'Brothers with travling certifcat 2*s* 0*d*' and in Feb. 1842 paid 'to a Brother Forestre in his travil 3*s* 0*d*'. AOF Hutton Cranswick minute and proposition book 1839-69; Minute book of Rising Star Lodge, IOOF MU, Beverley 1856-67, Oddfellows Hall, Beverley 1980.
46. Ibid., IOOF MU Triumph lodge, travelling card of John Hepton, 1869.
47. *HA*, 10/5/1839.
48. *Rules of the Loyal St Peter's Lodge, IOOF MU* [Lund] (Beverley, 1858) p. 3. In 1899 Mrs Bosanquet wrote as follows of the working-class funeral: 'The greatest festival of all is perhaps the funeral . . . the poverty of the family makes no difference in their eagerness, and the little nest-egg which a man has provided to help his wife through the first months of widowhood is often lavished within a few days of his death. I have known a woman have a hearse with four horses, and a carriage and a pair, for her husband's funeral, and within two weeks apply to the Guardians to feed her children', Mrs B. Bosanquet, *Rich and Poor* (London, 1899) p. 126 quoted in A. Wilson and H. Levy, *Burial Reform and Funeral Costs* (London, 1938) p. 75. A number of courts and lodges also seemingly paid for the gravestones of members with the orders emblem cut on them, a collection of at least six such gravestones to Oddfellows in Old Clee churchyard, S. Humberside. In Middleton on the Wolds churchyard is a gravestone to Thomas Garrett, died Jan. 1850 aged 24 which

Notes for pages 83-5

has on it a Foresters' horn and the motto 'Unitas, benevolentia et concordia', and the Middleton AOF court minute book has an entry on 1 Mar 1850 recording the proposal 'for the Court to bear the expence of the Foresters Arms being cut in a headstone for the late Brother Thomas Garrett'.

49. J. Morley, *Death, Heaven and the Victorians*, (London, 1971) p. 118; *HN* 4/7/1885. I owe this reference to Sue Neave.
50. Mss. burial book of Wm Carlill of Long Riston, joiner, in possession of Mrs Fewson of Benningholme Grange, 1978.
51. Gilbert, *The Evolution of National Insurance*, pp. 159-232, 289-447; idem, 'The Decay of Nineteenth Century Provident Institutions', 552-63; Treble, 'The Attitudes of Friendly Societies', 266-99. The minute books of East Riding village friendly societies contain very little on the moves to introduce state pensions and sickness benefits. In May 1897 Hutton Cranswick Oddfellows instructed their delegate to the IOOF MU annual meeting 'to oppose any scheme of state aid that would in any way interfere with the content of the funds of friendly societies', IOOF MU Hutton Cranswick minute book 1/5/1897. There was much discussion however of the National Insurance Act before and after it was passed, minute books: AOF Hutton Cranswick 20/5/1911, Lockington 8/1/1912, HCRO IOOF MU Elloughton district 29/6/1912, Elloughton lodge 12/1 - 8/6/1912.
52. Horn, 'Old Age', p. 373.
53. Employers contributed 3*d* a week and the state 2*d*. Gilbert, *The Evolution of National Insurance*, p. 350.
54. Rowntree and Kendall, pp. 219-20.
55. *Amendments of Rules and Tables from 12 July 1912 of the Loyal Triumph Lodge, Beverley District of IOOF MU* (Beverley, 1922). In return for 3*d* a month he only got £10 on death and £5 on death of first wife but for 4*s* 9*d* he received 30*s* per week during first 26 weeks, and 15*s* per week during the remainder of sickness, (these benefits ceasing at 70 years of age), £40 on death and £20 on death of first wife.

Notes for pages 86-90

6. Respectability and Rural Friendly Societies

1. H. Perkin, *The Origins of Modern English Society 1780-1880* (London, 1981) p. 383.
2. G.D.H. Cole and R. Postgate, *The Common People* (London, 1976) p. 368.
3. B. Harrison, *Peaceable Kingdom* (Oxford, 1982) p. 178.
4. P. Bailey, 'Will the Real Bill Banks Please Stand Up', *Journal of Social History*, 12, 1978-9, 336-53; Harrison, *Peaceable Kingdom*, pp. 176-88.
5. Bailey, 'Will the Real Bill Banks'; Foster, *Class Struggle*; Crossick, *An Artisan Elite*; Gray, *The Labour Aristocracy*; Tholfsen, *Working-class Radicalism*; Kirk, *The Growth of Working Class Reformism*.
6. Foster does not see friendly societies as a vehicle for embourgeoisement; they are classed along with pubs as part of traditional working-class culture, Foster, *Class Struggle*, p. 223.
7. E. Hobsbawm, 'The Aristocracy of Labour Reconsidered' in E. Hobsbawm, *Worlds of Labour* (London, 1984) pp. 242-3; Kirk, p. 175.
8. Ibid., p. 181.
9. Ibid., p. 180.
10. Quoted in Report of Registrar of Friendly Societies 1862, PP 1863, (449) XXIX p. 39.
11. *YG*, 6/5/1854 reference from Rex Russell.
12. H. Cunningham, *Leisure in the Industrial Revolution* (London, 1980) p. 122; Obelkevich, *Religion and Rural Society*, pp. 87-9.
13. Ibid., p. 89.
14. Howkins, *Whitsun*, pp. 19-20, 44; idem, 'The Taming of Whitsun', 194, 197-8, 200-2.
15. *DT*, 22/6/1861.
16. Ibid., 24/6/1865.
17. E. and S. Yeo, 'Ways of seeing: control and leisure versus class and struggle', in Yeo (eds), *Popular Culture*, p. 139.
18. For contemporary descriptions of drunkenness and fighting at mid-Victorian club feasts see M. Fuller, *West Country Friendly Societies*, pp. 114-16 and A. Howkins, *Whitsun*, pp. 39-42.

Notes for pages 90-2

19. *HA*, 12/6/1840.
20. Ibid., 12/7/1850.
21. *YG*, 13/7/1872.
22. IOOF MU Hutton Cranswick lodge fine book; AOF Middleton minute book.
23. Harrison, *Drink and the Victorians*, p. 53; Crossick, *Artisan Elite*, p. 178.
24. AOF *Directory*, 1850.
25. Statistics compiled from Neave, thesis, Appendix 1.
26. *Report of the Committee on Intemperance for the Convocation of the Province of York* (Church of England Temperance Society, Manchester, 1874) pp. 72-5.
27. Harrison, *Peaceable Kingdom*, p. 180.
28. Bailey, 'Will the Real Bill Banks', p. 342.
29. Plough plays were still common in and around South Cave in the late 1820s-early 1830s. Robert Sharp noted in his diary on 2 January 1832 'Almost every day there are parties or sets of Plough Boys going about with their trumpery music and rattling drum, and what they get given they spend for the good of the publicans and for their own ill - there wants a reform here', HCRO DDX/216. For a description of East Riding plough plays see M.C.F. Morris, *The British Workman*, (Cambridge, 1928) pp. 54-5.
30. I. Carter, *Farmlife in Northeast Scotland 1840-1914*, (Edinburgh, 1979) pp. 154-6; G.E. Evans, *The Horse in the Furrow* (London, 1960) pp. 245-50.
31. *HA*, 2/8/1839.
32. Ibid. 11/12/1840.
33. *Stamford Mercury*, 20/2/1846.
34. *Methodist Magazine*, 1813, pp. 66-71, quoted in R.C. Russell, 'Methodist Friendly Societies in Lincolnshire: the need for research on these', *Journal of the Lincolnshire Methodist History Society*, vol. 3, no. 6, Spring 1983, 124-5.
35. AOF Lockington minute book.
36. AOF Hutton Cranswick minute book.
37. The Revd Frances J. Lundy at Moulton, Lincs., in June 1851, commenting on the congregation at a friendly society service wrote

Notes for pages 92-4

in his diary: 'a more indevout set of people I never saw - not a response, 2 of them drunk - a very unencouraging affair it was. They had some bad music and a worse than lukewarm set they are. I was asked to dine with them but their misconduct disgusted me so much that I would not go.' A month earlier he had not been much more impressed when he preached at the club anniversary at his home village of Lockington, East Riding: 'Up at 5 and set to work at my Sermon. Before 10 it was finished when I breakfasted. Mr. Blanchard came and about 11 a wretched brass band, with the Foresters. Not many came and I gave them "a word spoken in due season". May it not be in vain! Collection 17/-. After service we dined, a party of 60 at Willson's Tavern, good dinner, lots of speechifying and bad music and Bakky. We dispersed at 4', mss. diary of Revd F.J. Lundy, 1851, typescript in possession of D. Neave. The earlier local societies had made payments out of club funds for the sermon and to church officials but the affiliated orders in contrast looked for a donation from the preacher. The rules of the Beverley Brotherly Society of 1828 allowed a guinea to the clergyman for the sermon, 10*s* to the organist, 10*s* 6*d* to the singers, and 2*s* each to the ringers, clerk, sexton and vergers, PRO FS 1/795 Yorks 7. When Lundy preached at Lockington in 1851 he donated 10*s* to club funds; earlier in May 1844 when the Revd William Proctor had preached he had donated 2*s* 6*d*. Lockington AOF minute book 1840-85.

38. Neave, *East Riding Friendly Societies*, pp. 28-9.
39. Yeo (eds), *Popular Culture* p. 158.
40. *HA*, 29/6/1849.
41. Ibid., 21/6/39; *Foresters' Miscellany*, 1841, p. 144.
42. *HA*, 31/5, 21/6, 2 and 30/8/1839, 24/7/1840, 28/5, 13/8/1841, 15/7/1842, 14 and 28/7/1843, 3/5, 26/7/1844, 4/7/1845, *YG* 1 and 22/6/1839.
43. AOF Hutton Cranswick minute book; *HN* 19/6/1886; *BG*, 26/6/75, 26/6/86.
44. Obelkevich, *Religion and Rural Society*, p. 89.
45. Bailey, 'Will the Real Bill Banks', p. 348.
46. Wilkinson, *Mutual Thrift*, p. 173; C.F. Rogers, *Principles of Parish*

Notes for pages 94-5

Work (London, 1905) pp. 108-9. For a fuller discussion of Anglican clergy and friendly societies see D. Neave, 'Anglican Clergy and Affiliated Order Friendly Societies' in E. Royle (ed.) *Regional Studies in the History of Religion in Britain since the Later Middle Ages* (Hull, 1986) pp. 182-90.

47. *Parish Magazine Union*, July 1897, p. 15, Mar. 1905, p. 6, Aug. 1905 p. 190, July 1907, p. 174.
48. See footnote 10 above; C. Booth, *The Aged Poor in England and Wales* (London, 1894) p. 405.
49. The 1884 Act changed the whole nature of rural politics; no longer could a member or candidate reach a major portion of the electorate by speaking, or appearing, at a few agricultural meetings in the local market towns. The farmers' political power diminished as that of the rural labourer and artisan increased. The focus of rural politics shifted from the town to the village. Soon after the passing of the Act J.W. Lowther wrote to Sir Stafford Northcote complaining, 'every petty hamlet expects its member or members to pay annual visits in person as well as contribute to its local charities, etc., etc.'. Salisbury (Hatfield) Papers, Lowther to Northcote, 20 Nov. 1884 quoted in R.J. Olney, 'The Politics of Land', in Mingay, *The Victorian Countryside*, vol. 1, p. 67. This pursuit of candidates for subscriptions to local charities and organisations was also complained of by Rider Haggard who contested Norfolk East as a Unionist in 1895 - 'From the moment a candidate appears in the field he is fair game, and every man's hand is in his pocket. Demands for "your patronage and support" fall on him, thick as leaves in Vallombrosa', H. Rider Haggard, *The Days of My Life*, vol. ii (London, 1926) p. 115 quoted in H. Pelling, *Social Geography of British Elections 1885-1910* (London, 1967) p. 11. Lord Francis Hervey, a former M.P. for Bury St Edmunds 1885-92 detailed these charitable subscriptions to his nephew, the prospective candidate, in 1904: 'The major things were in the nature of capital expenditure I think - a mission hall to be erected; church repaired; organ provided: important alterations to hospital; minor things, ordinary contributions to football and cricket club;

Notes for pages 95-8

sports at the Grammar School . . . ; prizes to schools £1 a year or in small cases 10/-; Friendly Societies and their outings . . . Then there would be a certain number of eleemosynary subscriptions . . .' ibid. The candidates became fair game for the friendly societies who sought both their financial support and their attendance and speeches at the feast days. In return the candidates needed the feast day as possibly the only occasion when he would reach the bulk of the newly enfranchised rural householders.

50. National United Order of Free Gardeners, *Annual Returns, Directory and Reference Book*, 1913.
51. R. Adelson, *Mark Sykes: portrait of an amateur* (London, 1975); S. Leslie, *Mark Sykes: his life and letters* (London, 1923); B. English, 'On the eve of the Great Depression: The economy of the Sledmere estate 1869-78', *Business History*, vol. 25, 1982, 24; *HN*, 21/8/1920; *Hull Daily Mail*, 18/8/1920; *BG*, 21/8/1920; *Pocklington Weekly News*, 14/6/1919; R.W.S. Craig, *British Parliamentary Elections 1885-1918* (London, 1974) p. 424.
52. *HN*, 29/5, 5/6, 12/6, 19/6, 26/6, 3/7, 10/7/1909; *Pocklington Weekly News*, 3/7/1909; HUL DDSY (2) 2/3 Mark Sykes engagement diary 1909.
53. *HN*, 12/6/1909; *Pocklington Weekly News*, 3/7/1909.
54. Kirk, *The Growth of Working Class Reformism*, p. 181.
55. R.J. Morris, 'The Labour Aristocracy in the British Class Struggle', *Refresh*, 7, 1988, 3.
56. Bailey, 'Will the Real Bill Banks', 338.

Conclusion

1. For an interesting example of traditional ritual being combined with the ceremonial of affiliated order feast days see D. Bathe, 'Oddfellows and Morris Dancing in a Peak District village', *Folk Music Journal*, 5, 1985, 4-47.
2. Howkins, *Poor Labouring Men* pp. 51-2 and plate 2.3. For example George Edwards, General Secretary of the Norfolk and Norwich Amalgamated Labour Union was an active member of the Foresters and Shepherds, and Zacharias Walker, agent for the

Notes for pages 98-100

National Agricultural Labourers' Union, was secretary of an Oddfellows lodge. Both these men gave evidence on friendly societies to the Royal Commission on the Aged Poor, Royal Commission on the Aged Poor, PP 1895, [C. 7684-1] XIV, pp. 349-70.

3. Armstrong, *Stability and Change*, p. 65.
4. Kirk, *The Growth of Working Class Reformism*, pp. 136-7.
5. J.M. Bellamy and J. Saville (eds), *Dictionary of Labour Biography*, vols. 1-2 (London, 1972-4).
6. D.J.V. Jones, *The Last Rising: The Newport Insurrection of 1839* (Oxford, 1985) pp. 30, 108.
7. Yeo (eds), *Popular Culture* pp. 159-60; J. Epstein and D. Thompson, *The Chartist Experience* (London, 1982) p. 327.
8. *Northern Star*, 21/11/1840, 2/1, 4 and 18/12/1841.

Appendix A. Origins and Early Development of the Chief Affiliated Orders

1. The largest nineteenth-century friendly societies not dealt with in this section are the National Independent Order of Oddfellows, the Nottingham Ancient Imperial United Order of Oddfellows, and the British Order of Ancient Free Gardeners. For these see Stead, *Short History*; 6th Annual Abstract of Labour Statistics PP 1900 [Cd 119] lxxxiii, pp. 52-3 and 16th Annual Abstract of Labour Statistics PP 1914 [Cd 7131] lxxx, p. 266. Although sometimes classed with the affiliated order friendly societies the Royal Antediluvian Order of Buffaloes [RAOB] was not, and is not, a self-help benefit society, M.W. Payne, *The Origin and Development of the Royal Antediluvian Order of Buffaloes* (Royal Antediluvian Order of Buffaloes, Grand Lodge of England, 1973) p. 140. Similarly the Independent Order of Good Templars [OGT] is solely a temperance society introduced from America in 1868, G.P. Williams and G.T. Brake, *Drink in Great Britain 1900-1979* (London, 1980) pp. 238-9. For more on the order in America see J.G. Woolley and W.E. Johnson, *Temperance Progress of the Century* (Toronto, 1903).
2. London in the Eighteenth century abounded with a great range of

Notes for pages 100-3

drinking clubs for all sections of society, see M.D. George, *London Life in the Eighteenth Century* (Harmondsworth, 1966), pp. 266-7; T. Burke, *English Night Life* (London, 1941) pp. 50-61.
3. J. Spry, *History of Oddfellowship* (London, 1867) pp. 187-8.
4. *Independent Order of Odd Fellows 1810-1975* (Manchester, 1975) p. [1]; R.W. Moffrey, 'Rise and Progress of the Manchester Unity 1810-1904' in E.L. Jones and D. Hudson, (eds), *Independent Order of Oddfellows Manchester Unity, Friendly Society Souvenir Manchester AMC* (Manchester, 1904) pp. 34-5; Sheffield Public Library, Beauchief Mss 971-4 Committee Minutes of Amicable Lodge, Sheffield, Aug. 4 1804.
5. *Independent Order of Odd Fellows 1810-1975* pp. [2-3].
6. Wilkinson, *Mutual Thrift*, pp. 69-70; Hardwick, *The History, Present Position*, p. 22; Gosden, *Friendly Societies*, pp. 31, 33.
7. *Friendly Societies Almanack and Diary* (Hull, 1895).
8. Sheffield Public Library, Beauchief Mss., BM 971/4.
9. J. Thornley, *History of the Grand United Order of Oddfellows*, Pt 1. (Manchester, 1911) p. 21.
10. Stead, *Short History*, p. 23.
11. Ibid., p. 24; Wilkinson, *Mutual Thrift*, p. 160.
12. 16th Annual Abstract of Labour Statistics PP 1914 [Cd 7131] lxxx, p. 266.
13. W.G. Cooper, *The Ancient Order of Foresters' Friendly Society 150 years 1834-1984* (Southampton, 1984) p. 2; see also T.B. Stead, 'Historical Sketch of the Order', in *Directory of the Ancient Order of Foresters' Friendly Society 1896* (Dundee, 1896) pp. vii-xxxviii; 'Historical Sketch of the Order', in *Directory of the Ancient Order of Foresters' Friendly Society 1978* (Southampton, 1978) pp. v-lxiv; J.F. Wilkinson, *The Friendly Society Movement* (London, 1886).
14. Stead, *Short History*, p.16.
15. Cooper, *The Ancient Order of Foresters*, pp. 8-9, 17; 'Historical Sketch . . .', 1978, p. viii.
16. T.B. Stead, *Directory of the Ancient Order of Foresters' Friendly Society for 1896* (Dundee, 1896) p. 624.
17. F. Askew, 'Rise and Revival of the United Ancient Order of Druids',

Notes for pages 103-5

UAOD Quarterly Magazine, 1900, pp. 228-32, 274; R.S. Brooks, *Essay on the Friendly Societies in England,* (UAOD n.d.) p. 2.; *Directory and Diary of the United Ancient Order of Druids Friendly Society 1938* (Hull, 1937) p. 20; Stead, *Short History*, p. 30.

18. Askew, 'Rise and Revival', p. 274; *The Order of Druids Almanack 1864* (Manchester, 1864); HCRO DDML 12/10 *Book on Constitutional Laws of the United Ancient Order of Druids and Rules for Government of the Hull District* 1861.
19. *Directory and Diary of UAOD 1938* p. 9; *Order of Druids Directory 1914* (Manchester, 1914).
20. Crew, *Loyal Order of Ancient Shepherds Friendly Society*, pp. 5-15, 41-2; D.H. Hague, *Historical Sketch of The Loyal Order of Ancient Shepherds* (Stockport, *c.*1967), pp. 2-4, 13; E. Crew, 'Foundation and Progress to the Present Day of the Loyal Order of Ancient Shepherds (Ashton Unity)' in *The Loyal Order of Ancient Shepherds Guide and Directory 1923-1924*, pp. iv-vi; Stead, *Short History*, pp. 34-6. The LOAS was unique amongst the non-temperance affiliated orders in having associated with it female lodges, the first female branch being opened at Rochdale in 1829. There was, apparently, a Loyal Order of Ancient Shepherdesses independent of the parent body but it was beset by rifts and information on the various female orders is limited, ibid., Crew, *Loyal Order of Ancient Shepherds Friendly Society*, p. 74.
21. Stead, *Short History*, pp. 45-6.
22. Ibid., pp. 45-50; H.T. Finch, *History of the Order* (NUOFG, Dudley, 1900); *National United Order of Free Gardeners Friendly Society Short History* (Sandbach, n.d.).
23. This section on Rechabites is from Campbell, *Rechabite History* pp. 3-39, 47-8, 73, 120, 150-1, 162, 173, 219-27; Highet, *Rechabite History* (Manchester, 1936) pp. 7-27, 501; Stead, *Short History*, pp. 93-4.
24. Ibid., p. 100.
25. Ibid., pp. 100-2; *The Son of Temperance*, Vol. III No. 36, Oct. 1884.
26. Ibid.; Wilkinson, *Mutual Thrift*, p. 161; see table 18.

Notes for pages 107-11

Appendix B. Primary Sources for a Regional Study of Friendly Societies

1. The accession of friendly society records to county and other archive collections is reported in the annual list of archive deposits in the *Society for the Study of Labour History Bulletin.*
2. Neave, 'The Local Records of Affiliated Friendly Societies', *Local Historian,* 16 1984, 161-7. For an account of a similar search for labour archives see J. Harper, 'Labour Archives in the Calder Valley', *History Workshop,* 5, 1978, pp. 147-54; see also 'Labour Archives: a guide to their location and preservation', *Society for the Study of Labour History Bulletin,* 36, 1978, pp. 3-6.
3. A fuller account of the documentary sources is contained in Neave, thesis, pp. 12-34.
4. R.L.M. James, 'The Records of Friendly Societies', *Archives,* 6, 1964, pp. 223-4.
5. Gosden made particular use of two large London collections in Goldsmiths' Library, University of London and the British Library, Gosden, *Friendly Societies,* pp. 245-6.
6. The extent of nineteenth-century printed and manuscript material surviving at the headquarters of the chief affiliated orders varies enormously. The AOF has a well maintained collection of early printed material consisting of almost complete runs of its annual and quarterly reports, directories and magazines for 1834. Almost nothing however survives for the UAOD and apparently nothing at all for the IOOF KU.
7. Similar annual reports are available for the IOR from 1837, the LOAS from 1838, and the NUOFG from 1851. The GUOOF have quarterly reports 1848-9, then from 1856.
8. Gosden, *Friendly Societies,* between pp. 132-3; *List of Lodges* 1845 in Manchester Central Library; 1850 in Grimsby Library. Lists of the lodges in the NUOFG are included in the printed annual returns from 1851. For the other orders the earliest discovered directories at order headquarters are as follows: GUOOF, 1880; IOR, 1888; LOAS, 1890; UAOD, 1938. A list of UAOD lodges in 1862 is incorporated in a copy of the *Laws of*

Notes for page 111-13

the UAOD in HCRO DDML 12/10.

9. *DT* 27/6/1874 in report on Harpham Druids' feast.
10. Russell, *Friendly Societies in the Caistor, Binbrook and Brigg Area.*

Select Bibliography

1. Printed Works on Friendly Societies

Askew, F.	'Rise and Revival of the United Ancient Order of Druids', *United Ancient Order of Druids Magazine*, vol. 2, 1899-1901, 228-33, 272-7, 322-7.
Baernreither, J.M.	*English Associations of Working Men* (London, 1889).
Bathe, D.	'Oddfellows and Morris Dancing in a Peak District village', *Folk Music Journal*, 5, 1985, 4-47.
Brabrook, E.W.	*Provident Societies and Industrial Welfare* (London, 1898).
Brabrook, E.W.	'Friendly Societies and Similar Institutions', *Journal of the Statistical Society*, 38, 1875, 185-206.
Brabrook, E.W.	'The Relation of the State to Thrift: ten years statistics of friendly societies and similar institutions', *Journal of the Statistical Society*, 48, 1885, 21-44.
Brabrook, E.W.	'The Progress of Friendly Societies and other Institutions connected with the Friendly Societies Registry Office during the Ten Years 1884-94', *JRSS*, 58, 1895, 286-302.
Brabrook, E.W.	'On the Progress of Friendly Societies and other Institutions connected with the Friendly Societies Registry Office during the Ten Years 1894-1904', *JRSS*, 68, 1905, 320-42.
Brabrook, E.W.	'On the Progress of Friendly Societies and other Provident Institutions during the Ten Years 1904-1914', *JRSS*, 78, 1915, 414-33.
Brooks, R.S.	*Essay on the Friendly Societies in England* (United Ancient Order of Druids, n.d.).
Brown, S.J.	'Friendly Societies and their Symbols and Ritual', *Group for Regional Studies in Museums Journal* 10, Oct. 1982, 7-11.
Campbell, R.	*Rechabite History: a record of the origin, rise*

and progress of the Independent Order of Rechabites Salford Unity (Manchester, 1911).

Campbell, R. *Provident and Industrial Institutions* (Manchester, n.d. [*c*. 1925]).

Cooper, W.G. *The Ancient Order of Foresters' Friendly Society 150 years 1834-1984* (Southampton, 1984).

Crew, E. *Loyal Order of Ancient Shepherds' Friendly Society A.U.: Centenary Souvenir 1826-1926* (Manchester, 1926).

Davis, P. *The Old Friendly Societies of Hull* (Hull, 1926).

Fierke, F.W. 'The Rise and Progress of Friendly Societies in Hull' in *Souvenir Handbook of The National Conference of Friendly Societies* (Hull, 1915).

Fierke, F.W. (ed.) *The Order of the Sons of Temperance Friendly Society Hull Grand Division Jubilee Souvenir 1865-1915* (Hull, 1915).

Finch, H.T. *History of the Order* (National United Order of Free Gardeners, Dudley, 1900).

Finch, J. 'Twyford's Friendly Societies', *Berkshire Old and New*, Berkshire Local History Association, 5, 1988, 18-26.

'Forestry in Hull and Neighbourhood', *Directory of the Ancient Order of Foresters* 1890, xlv-vii.

Fuller, M. *West Country Friendly Societies* (Reading, 1964).

Gilbert, B.B. 'The Decay of Nineteenth-century Provident Institutions and the coming of Old Age Pensions in Great Britain' *Economic History Review* 17, 1964-65, 551-63.

Gosden, P.H.J.H. *The Friendly Societies in England 1815-1875* (Manchester, 1963).

Gosden, P.H.J.H. *Self-Help: voluntary associations in nineteenth-century Britain* (London, 1973).

Hagerty, J.M. 'Bradford Friendly Societies in the 1790s', *Bradford Antiquary*, 1976, 45-64.

Hague, D. *Historical Sketch* (The Loyal Order of Ancient Shepherds' (Ashton Unity) Friendly Society, 1967).

Hardwick, C. *The History, Present Position, and Social Importance of Friendly Societies* (3rd ed., London, 1893).

Highet, R. *Rechabite History* (Independent Order of Rechabites, Salford Unity, Manchester, 1936).

Hobsbawm, E.J. 'Friendly Societies', *Amateur Historian*, 3, 1957, 95-101.

Hothersall, G. 'Friendly Societies in West Sussex 1794-1875', *West Sussex History*, 35, Sept. 1986, 18-22; 36, Jan. 1987, 12-18; 37, May 1987, 25-30.

Independent Order of Odd Fellows Manchester Unity Friendly Society 1810-1975 (Independent Order of Odd Fellows, Manchester, 1975).

James, R.L.M. 'The Records of Friendly Societies', *Archives*, 6, 1964, 223-4.

Jones, D. 'Did Friendly Societies matter?: A study of friendly societies in Glamorgan 1794-1910', *Welsh History Review*, 12, 1985, 324-49.

Maltby, H.J.M. 'Early Bradford Friendly Societies', *Bradford Antiquary*, 1921, 17-28.

Matthews, R.D. *Friendly Societies and their Origins* (Leeds, 1935).

Moffrey, R.W. 'Rise and Progress of the Manchester Unity 1810-1904' in E.L. Jones and D. Hudson, *Souvenir Manchester A.M.C., Independent Order of Oddfellows, Manchester Unity Friendly Society* (Manchester, 1904) 31-109.

Moffrey, R.W. *A Century of Oddfellowship* (Manchester, 1910).

Moulton, J.E. 'Ungodly Associations Exposed', *Wesleyan Methodist Magazine*, 1841, 302-5.

National United Order of Free Gardeners Friendly Society Short History (Sandbach, n.d.).

Neave, D. 'The Local Records of Affiliated Friendly Societies', *Local Historian*, 16, 1984, 161-9.

Neave, D. 'Victorian Self-help and the Local Community', *Local History*, 1, 1984, 10-11.

Neave, D. 'Anglican Clergy and Affiliated Order Friendly Societies', in E. Royle (ed.), *Regional Studies in the History of Religion in Britain since the Later*

Middle Ages (Hull, 1986) 182-190.

Neave, D. *Feasts, Fellowship and Financial Aid: South Holderness friendly societies* (Beverley, 1986).

Neave, D. *East Riding Friendly Societies* (Beverley, 1988).

Neison, F.G.P. 'Some Statistics of the Affiliated Orders of Friendly Societies (Odd Fellows and Foresters)', *Journal of Statistical Society* 40, 1877, 42-89.

O'Neill, J. 'Self-Help in Nottinghamshire: The Woodborough male friendly society, 1926-1954', *Transactions of the Thoroton Society*, 90, 1986, 57-63.

O'Neill, J. 'A Search for Independence?: Friendly societies in Nottinghamshire 1724-1912', *Bulletin of Local History East Midland Region*, 13, 1988, 11-15.

Prichard, M.F.Ll. 'Friendly Societies in Norfolk 1700-1850', *Notes and Queries* 201, 401-4; 206, 252-4.

Russell, R.C. *Friendly Societies in the Caistor, Binbrook and Brigg Area in the 19th Century* (Nettleton, 1975).

Russell, R.C. 'Methodist Friendly Societies in Lincolnshire - the need for Research on these', *Journal of the Lincolnshire Methodist History Society* 3, 1983, 123-5.

Shaw, J.W. *Historical Notes on the Order of Druids* (Order of Druids, Manchester, 1936).

Smiles, S. 'Workmen's Benefit Societies', *Quarterly Review*, 116, 1864, 318-50.

Sons of Temperance of Great Britain and Ireland Friendly Society 1855-1955 (Sons of Temperance, 1955).

Spry, J. *History of Odd-Fellowship* (London, 1867).

Stead, T.B. *A Short History of the Chief Affiliated Friendly Societies* (Leeds, 1880).

Storey, T.H. 'The Oddfellows Hall, Grimsby, and its Place in the Social Life of the Town', *Lincolnshire History and Archaeology*, 12, 1977, 49-54.

Stratton, J.Y. 'Farm Labourers, their Friendly Societies and the Poor Law', *Journal of the Royal Agricultural*

Society of England, 31, 1870, 87-119.

Stratton, J.Y. 'Friendly Societies, State Action, and the Poor Law', *Journal of the Royal Agricultural Society of England*, 43, 1882, 153-86.

Thornley, J. *History of the Grand United Order of Oddfellows* 3 vols (Manchester, 1911-13).

Treble, J.H. 'The Attitudes of Friendly Societies towards the Movement in Great Britain for State Pensions 1878-1908', *International Review of Social History*, 15, 1970, 266-99.

Turner, J.J. 'The Growth and Development of Friendly Societies in Cleveland and Teesside *c.* 1835-1914: a preliminary research note', *Cleveland and Teesside Local History Society Bulletin*, 48, spring 1985, 22-36.

Walford, C. 'Friendly Societies', in *Insurance Cyclopaedia* vol. iv (London, 1870-8) 379-616.

Wilkinson, J.F. *The Friendly Society Movement* (London, 1886).

Wilkinson, J.F. *Mutual Thrift* (London, 1891).

2. Secondary Printed Sources

Allison, K.J. (ed.) *Victoria County History: East Riding*, vol. 2 (London, 1974), vol. 5 (London, 1984).

Armstrong, A. *Stability and Change in an English County Town: A social study of York* (Cambridge, 1974).

Bailey, P. 'Will the Real Bill Banks Please Stand Up', *Journal of Social History*, 12, 1978-9, 336-53.

Best, G. *Mid-Victorian Britain 1851-75* (London, 1971).

Bulmer, T. *History and Directory of East Yorkshire* (Preston, 1892).

Bushaway, B. *By Rite: custom, ceremony and community in England 1700-1880* (London, 1982).

Crossick, G. *An Artisan Elite in Victorian Society* (London, 1978).

Cunningham, H. *Leisure in the Industrial Revolution* (London, 1980).

Dunbabin, J.P. 'The Incidence and Organization of Agricultural Trades Unionism in the 1870s', *Agricultural*

History Review, xvi, 1968, 114-141.

Eddowes, J. *Martinmas Musings: or, thoughts about the hiring-day* (Driffield, 1854).

Everitt, A. *The Pattern of Rural Dissent: the nineteenth century* (Leicester, 1972).

Foster, J. *Class Struggle and the Industrial Revolution* (London, 1977).

Gilbert, B.B. *The Evolution of National Insurance in Great Britain* (London, 1966).

Gray, R.Q. 'Styles of Life, the 'Labour Aristocracy' and Class Relations in Later Nineteenth Century Edinburgh', *International Review of Social History*, 18, 1973, 428-52.

Gray, R.Q. *The Labour Aristocracy in Victorian Edinburgh* (Oxford, 1976).

Green, D.G. *Working-Class Patients and the Medical Establishment* (Aldershot, 1985).

Hanson, C.G. 'Welfare before the Welfare State', in R.M. Hartwell and others (eds), *The Long Debate on Poverty* (London, 1972) 113-39.

Harris, R.W. *National Health Insurance in Great Britain 1911-46* (London, 1946).

Harrison, B. *Peaceable Kingdom* (Oxford, 1982).

Hastings, R.P. *Essays in North Riding History 1780-1850* (Northallerton, 1981).

Hebden, C.D. *The Trustee Savings Banks of Yorkshire and Lincoln* (1981).

Hobsbawm, E.J. *Labouring Men* (London, 1968).

Hobsbawm, E.J. *Worlds of Labour* (London, 1984).

Hobsbawm, E.J. and Rudé, G. *Captain Swing* (Harmondsworth, 1973).

Hodgkinson, R.G. *The Origins of the National Health Service: the medical services of the New Poor Law 1834-1871* (London, 1967).

Horn, P. 'Old Age and the Oxfordshire Agricultural Labourer 1870-1914', *Oxoniensa*, 38, 1973, 373-80.

Horn, P. *Labouring Life in The Victorian Countryside* (Dublin, 1976).

Howkins, A. *Whitsun in 19th Century Oxfordshire* (Oxford, 1973).

Howkins, A. 'The Taming of Whitsun: the changing face of a nineteenth-century rural holiday' in E. and S. Yeo (eds) *Popular Culture and Class Conflict 1590-1914* (Brighton 1981) 187-207.

Howkins, A. *Poor Labouring Men: rural radicalism in Norfolk 1870-1923* (London, 1985).

Howorth, P. *Driffield 1700-1860* (Driffield, 1980).

Hunt, E.H. *Regional Wage Variations in Britain 1850-1914* (Oxford, 1973).

Johnson, P. 'Credit and Thrift and the Working Class', in J. Winter (ed.), *The Working Class in Modern British History* (Cambridge, 1983) 147-70.

Johnson, P. *Saving and Spending: the working-class economy in Britain 1870-1939* (Oxford, 1985).

Kirk, N. *The Growth of Working Class Reformism in Mid-Victorian England* (London, 1985).

Kussmaul, A. *Servants in Husbandry in Early Modern England* (Cambridge, 1981).

Leeson, R.A. *Travelling Brothers* (St Albans, 1979).

Marland, H. *Medicine and Society in Wakefield and Huddersfield 1780-1870* (Cambridge, 1987).

Mingay, G.E. (ed.) *The Victorian Countryside*, 2 vols (London, 1981).

Morris, F.O. *Possibilities in a Parish* (London, 1850).

Obelkevich, J. *Religion and Rural Society: South Lindsey 1825-75* (Oxford, 1976).

Perkin, H. *The Origins of Modern English Society 1780-1880* (London, 1981).

Ross, F. *Contributions towards a History of Driffield* (Driffield, 1898).

Rowntree, B.S. and Kendall, M. *How the Labourer lives* (London, 1913).

Sheahan, J.J. and Whellan, T. *History and Topography of the City of York and the East Riding of Yorkshire, vol. 2* (Beverley, 1856).

Sheppard, J.A. 'East Yorkshire's Agricultural Labour Force in the Mid-nineteenth Century', *Agricultural*

History Review, ix, 1961, 43-54.

Snell, K.D.M. *Annals of the Labouring Poor: social change and agrarian England 1660-1900* (Cambridge, 1985).

Thane, P. 'Non-contributory versus Insurance Pensions 1878-1908' in P. Thane (ed.), *The Origins of British Social Policy* (London, 1978) 84-106.

Thane, P. *The Foundations of the Welfare State* (London, 1982).

Tholfsen, T.R. *Working-Class Radicalism in Mid-Victorian England* (London, 1976).

Thompson, E.P. *The Making of the English Working Class* (Harmondsworth, 1968).

Ward, J.T. *East Yorkshire Landed Estates in the Nineteenth Century* (York, 1967).

White, W. *History, Gazetteer, and Directory of the East and North Ridings of Yorkshire* (Sheffield, 1840).

Wilson, A. and Levy, H. *Industrial Assurance* (London, 1937).

Woodcock, H. *Piety amongst the Peasantry* (London, 1889).

Yeo, E and S. (eds) *Popular Culture and Class Conflict 1590-1914* (Brighton, 1981).

Yeo, S. 'Working-class Association, Private Capital, Welfare and the State in the Late-nineteenth and Twentieth Centuries' in N. Parry, M. Rustin and C. Satyamuri (eds) *Social Work, Welfare and the State* (London, 1979) 48-71.

3. Theses and Dissertations

Adams, M.G. 'Agricultural Change in the East Riding of Yorkshire 1850-80' (Hull University, Ph.D., 1977).

Barnett, D.C. 'Ideas on Social Welfare, 1780-1834, with Special Reference to Friendly Societies and Allotment Schemes' (Nottingham University, M.A., 1961).

Brown, S. 'The Development of the Friendly Society' (Leeds University, M.A., 1976).

Bushrod, W.T. 'The Development of the Great Affiliated Friendly Societies' (Manchester University, M.A., 1924).

Crossick, G.J. 'Social Structure and Working-class Behaviour: Kentish London 1840-80' (London University, Ph.D., 1976).

Gosden, P.H.J.H. 'The Development of Friendly Societies in England 1815-75' (London University, Ph.D., 1959).

Hopkin, N.D. 'The Old and New Poor Law in East Yorkshire *c.* 1760-1850' (Leeds University, M.Phil., 1968).

Neave, D. 'Friendly Societies in the Rural East Riding 1830-1912' (Hull University, Ph.D., 1986).

Index

Places are in the East Riding of Yorkshire unless otherwise stated. Counties given are those prior to the 1974 reorganisation.